Pig in a Pen
and Other Fiddle Ditties For
Galax Dulcimer
and Other Hogfiddles
Phyllis & Jim Gaskins

Layout and Editing - Brent M. Holl
Illustrations and Cover Photos by Phyllis Gaskins
Associate Editor - Karen Holl
Printed and distributed by Fingers Of Steel
www.FingersOfSteel.com
© 2022 Phyllis Gaskins. All rights reserved.
ISBN 978-1-964725-57-4

WHY PIG IN A PEN?

Felts Park, 1976, Galax Fiddlers' Convention,
Camped in the back field of wet grassy green,
Far, far away from the music and stage,
No musician camping or famed jamming scene.

Musician camping, jamming near the stage,
Musicians summoned, competing at their peak,
Two and a half minutes of fame and a small fortune,
The refund of entry and camping fee for the week.

"Dear musicians, how can I camp with you?"
"Just enter a contest, play something tune-like and smile."
Two and a half minutes of fame and a small fortune,
Friendlier camping in the musicians' aisle.

Felts Park, 1977, Galax Fiddlers' Convention,
"Why, yes, I'm a registered contestant,
The mountain dulcimer is my instrument."
Enter musician camping, let jamming be persistent.

"All you dulcimer players come to the big 'yeller' tent."
"Yes, sir! Yes, sir! My tune is called *Pig in a Pen*."
Played a less than two-minute tune wonder,
Set me up for life with mountain dulcimer Zen.

CONTENTS

- 1 **Nutrition for the Hogfiddle Brain**
- 3 **D TUNES**
- 5 Can You Dance A Tobacco Hill?
- 6 Cheat River
- 7 Cousin Sally Brown
- 8 Down by the Salley Gardens
- 9 The Eighth of January
- 11 Grasshopper Sittin' on a Sweet Potato Vine
- 12 Lifting Fog
- 13 Lily of the Valley
- 14 Morpeth Rant
- 15 Nancy Blevins
- 16 Needlecase
- 17 Rocking My Babies to Sleep
- 19 Rock that Cradle, Joe
- 20 Trude Evans
- 21 Tucker's Barn
- 23 Twin Sisters
- 24 **G TUNES**
- 25 Barlow Knife
- 26 Billy in the Lowland
- 27 Cotton-Eyed Joe
- 28 Gentle Maiden
- 29 The Irish Washerwoman
- 30 Jamie Allen
- 31 Lost Girl
- 32 Magpie
- 33 Mulvahill's Polkas #1
- 34 Mulvahill's Polkas #2
- 35 Old Dad
- 36 Old Yeller Dog Came Trottin' Through the Meetin' House
- 37 Pear Tree
- 38 Pig in a Pen
- 39 Piney Woods Gal
- 40 Prettiest Little Girl in the County
- 41 Roscoe
- 42 Walking That Pretty Girl Home
- 43 Waves on the Ocean
- 44 The Deaf Woman's Courtship
- 45 **A-ish TUNES**
- 47 Betty Likens
- 48 Callahan
- 49 June Apple
- 50 Little Dutch Girl
- 51 Little Rabbit
- 53 Oh, Miss Liza, Poor Gal
- 54 Old Mother Flannagan
- 55 Ole Time John Henry
- 57 Red Haired Boy
- 58 Santa Anna's Retreat
- 59 Sourwood Mountain
- 60 Sullivan's Polka
- 61 Tater Patch
- 62 Undaunted Noter
- 63 Walsh's Hornpipe
- 65 **TWO-KEY TUNES**
- 66 Belfast Polka
- 67 Little Black Dog Came Trottin' Down the Road
- 68 Puncheon Floor
- 69 **EM TUNES**
- 70 Lanigan's Ball
- 71 Scollay's Reel
- 72 The Butterfly
- 73 **Hoeing The "Hogfiddle" Hills**
- 88 Home Now

> Videos of Jim and Phyllis playing many of the tunes in this book are available on their Vimeo Showcase.
> Tunes for You
> https://vimeo.com/showcase/7823477

NUTRITION FOR THE HOGFIDDLE BRAIN

(Questions Answered for Using This Book)

QUESTION: Does it matter which way you strum?

ANSWER: No and Yes.

NO: I use the IN strum to emphasize the first and third beats. According to your background and playing experience you may wish to use the OUT strum to emphasize the first and third beats. Sometimes I purposely use the OUT strum for emphasis on repetitive notes. If you are an OUT strummer, simply reverse the direction of the arrows when strumming.

YES: Keep the rhythm steady and regular by having a strum pattern that works for the flow of the tune's melody and rhythm. My style of playing has a very strong rhythmic feel to it. I include the strumming arrows because the strumming patterns affect the sound of the tunes played. There is a subtle difference in rhythm and tone between in-strumming and out-strumming. This may not be apparent to the novice, but it is important. The Galax dulcimer is not like other dulcimers and plectrum instruments (guitars, mandolins, etc.) which are strummed OUT from the bass to the treble. IN-strumming is the traditional way of playing this Old Virginia style dulcimer. Decide for yourself how closely to adhere to the tradition.

Use the traditional counting system to interpret the rhythm of each tune. Count each note value like the example below. In cut time, play the tune with a two-beat feel instead of a four-beat feel. The 6/8 time tunes also have a two-beat feel.

↓   Strum in toward your body.

↑   Strum out away from your body.

∨   Strum in, then out.

∧   Strum out, then in.

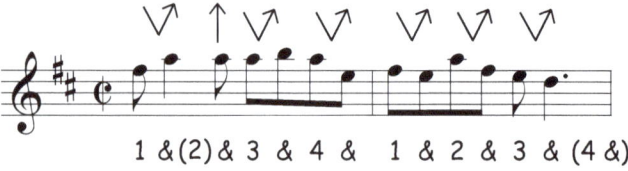

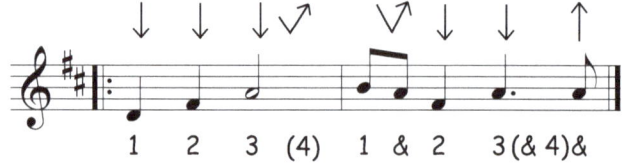

Q: What's this and what's it for?

A: It's a chord chart. If you have another instrument accompanying you, these chords can be used. Each box is a measure with either one or two chords per measure. The chart is divided into the parts of the tune by A, B, and in some cases C.

Chord Chart

A Part	D	G D	D	G D
B Part	D	G D	D	G D

Q: Why do the tunings have upper case and lower case letters?

A: The lower case d is the d beside of middle C on the piano. The D, A, and G are for the heavier gauge strings tuned to these notes below middle C on the piano. Any upper case letter indicates the note below middle C. Any lower case letters indicate notes above middle C.

D tunes Key: D Tuning: dddd or DAd	A tunes Key: A major (Ionian) Tuning: dddd, use false nut to make e drones or DGd capoed at the 1st fret to make EAe
G tunes Key: G Tuning: dddd or DGd	Key: A major (Gapped scale, no Gs) Tuning: dddd, use false nut to make e drones or DGd capoed at the 1st fret to make EAe.
Em tunes Key: Em Tuning: dddd, use false nut to make e drones or DAd capoed at the 1st fret to make EBe.	Key: A mixolydian (G naturals) Tuning: dddd, use false nut to make e drones or DGd capoed at the 1st fret to make EAe.

Early dulcimer capos were a stick of some sort attached tightly with rubber bands.

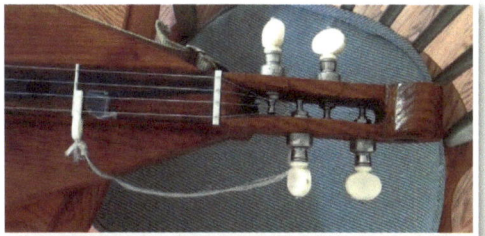

Modern Dulcimer Capo

False Nut Placement

The Galax dulcimer has four equidistant strings of the same gauge tuned to **b**eside middle C on the piano (dddd).

Tune the bass string to **D** below middle C.
Tune the middle string to **A** below middle C
Tune the first or first two strings to d beside middle C on the piano (DAd).

D TUNES

Imagine being the only dulcimer player walking into a room full of Old Time musicians tuning screechy, caterwauling banjos, fiddles, and various other stringed instruments.

ME: "How's the banjo tuned tonight, boys?"

GROUP: "D. We're in D."

METHINKS: Whew! I'm ready!

For the next two hours we play "D Tunes."

D TUNES: Fiddle tunes are referred to as D Tunes, G Tunes, A Tunes, etc., based on the preferred key for those particular fiddle tunes. The next few pages are D Tunes, so called because they are virtually always played in the key of D major by fiddlers.

NOTES: A note is a symbol that represents a musical tone or the name of that musical tone. In our local sessions we call them "little black dots."

SCALE: A **scale** is a sequence of seven notes that repeat in an ascending or descending order.

KEY: The **key** of a tune corresponds to the beginning note of the scale in which the tune is composed.

D is the **first note and the key note** of the D <u>major</u> scale.

    The scale: D E F# G A B C# D

So when we say we're in D, it means we are going to play tunes in the **key** of D.

D Tunes

TUNING: A tuning indicates the notes to which the strings are tuned. The tunings used in this section are:

1. **dddd** (Galax tuning)

2. **Dddd** (Bagpipe tuning)

3. **DAd** (This is called mixolydian tuning by many folks, but mixolydian is a mode, not a tuning.)

Because the D major scale has a C#, in any of the tunings above, one must have a fret between fret number 6 and fret number 7. This added fret is called the six-and-a-half, 6.5, or 6+. Dulcimers are diatonic instruments, meaning they do not have all 12 tones of the western chromatic scale. Today most dulcimers have a 6.5 fret which you need for the tunings in this book.

I have often heard DAd referred to as mixolydian so called because before dulcimers had the 6.5 fret, there would have been no C sharp on the dulcimer and the scale starting at the open string would be:

The D mixolydian scale (mode)...... D E F# G A B C D

The fret 0 1 2 3 4 5 6 7

The seventh tone would be C natural, not C sharp. The mixolydian scale always has a flatted seventh tone in relation to the major scale. Only a small number of D mixolydian tunes exist in the Old Time fiddle tradition.

IF you are tuned **dddd**, **Dddd** or **DAd**, then these are the fret numbers for the d scale. The D major scale (sometimes called D Ionian) is fretted on the frets in the second row.

IF you are tuned DAA, play the fret numbers on the bottom row.

D	E	F#	G	A	B	C#	D
0	1	2	3	4	5	6+	7
3	4	5	6	7	8	9	10

QUESTION: So, Ms. Phyllis, why are we talking about DAA tuning?

ANSWER: I mention **DAA** tuning because any of the these D Tunes can be played on the first string in DAA or the middle A string in DAd simply by adding 3 to each of the numbers listed under "the dots," or you can just "read the dots."

QUESTION: So, can four different dulcimers each tuned to one of the four tunings, DAd, Dddd, dddd, or DAA all play these tunes together at the same time?

ANSWER: Yes. Just remember, if you are tuned to DAA, or if you want to play on the middle string DAd tuning, then you must add 3 to each of the numbers for fretting.

BONUS POINT!
If you are tuned to DAd or Dddd, then you can use the numbers to play the tunes on the bass string. Like we used to say back in the '70s, "Dulcimers are Fun!"

D Tunes

CAN YOU DANCE A TOBACCO HILL?

Key: D
Tuning: dddd or DAd

Traditional

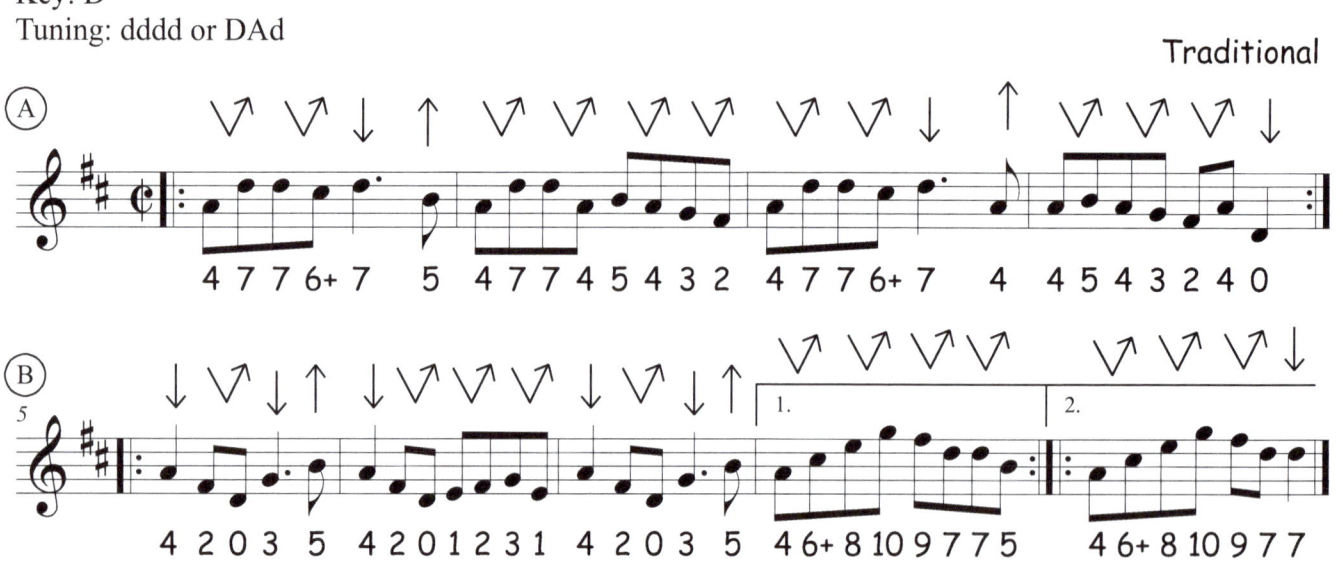

Chord Chart

Part A	D	D A	D	A D
Part B	D G	D A	D G	A D

Can You Dance a Tobacco Hill is called a single reel because each part has four measures basically repeated twice instead of the usual eight measures for each part. Look for more single reels in this book; they are easier to memorize.

Tobacco grows best in a sunny location with well-drained soil, so it is planted in rows called "hills." These rows are bedded upward with ditches dug between them to collect and remove excess water.

Granddaddy shook tobacco from the pouch onto a cigarette paper, closed the pouch, rolled the cigarette, licked the edge of the paper to seal the rolled cigarette, twisted the ends and had a good smoke. He used tobacco from the same pouch to fill his pipe. Over the years his hands aged like withered tobacco leaves.

D Tunes

CHEAT RIVER

Key: D
Tuning: dddd or DAd

Traditional

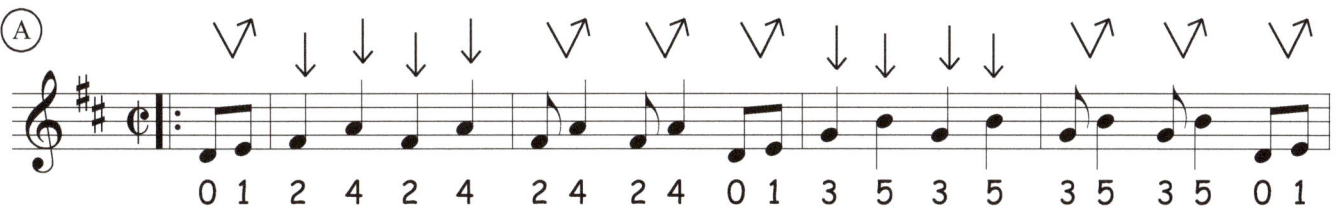
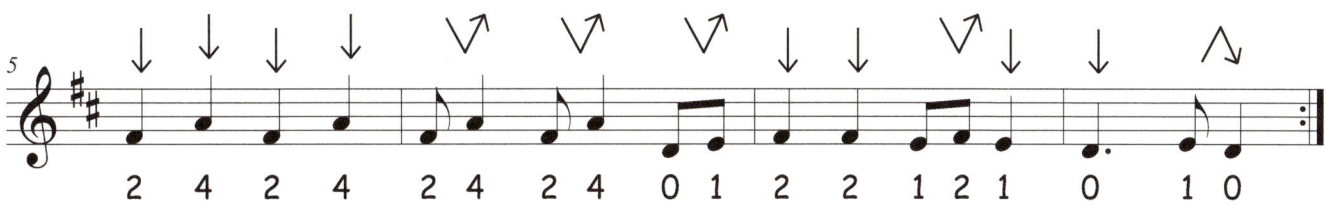
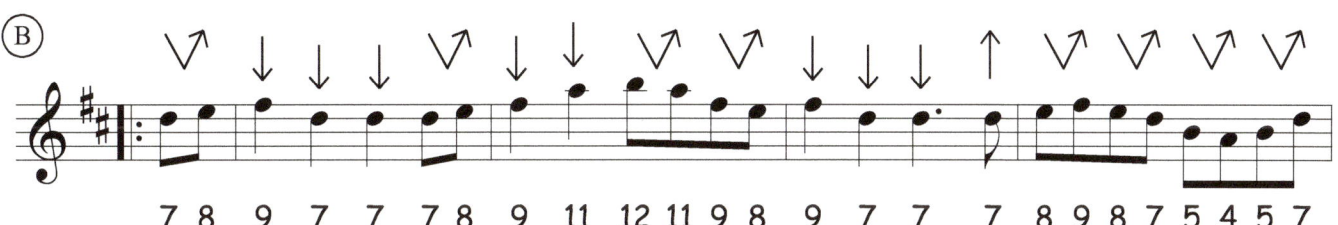
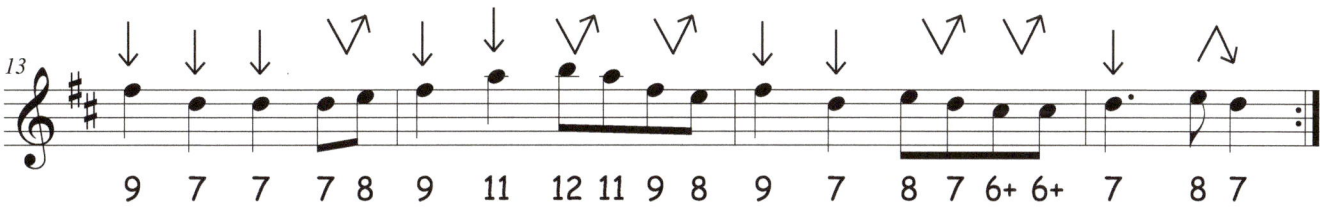

Source: Baity "Pap" Earl Ridder (1904 - 1989), Oakland, Maryland

Chord Chart				
Part A	D	D	G	G
	D	D	DA	D
Part B	D	D	D	A
	D	D	DA	D

Pap was the father of Gene White who taught reading next door to me at Keezletown Elementary. Jim and I met Pap at her house one Sunday afternoon and learned this rare gem of a tune from him.

Photo by Gene White

D Tunes

COUSIN SALLY BROWN

Key: D
Tuning: dddd or DAd

Traditional

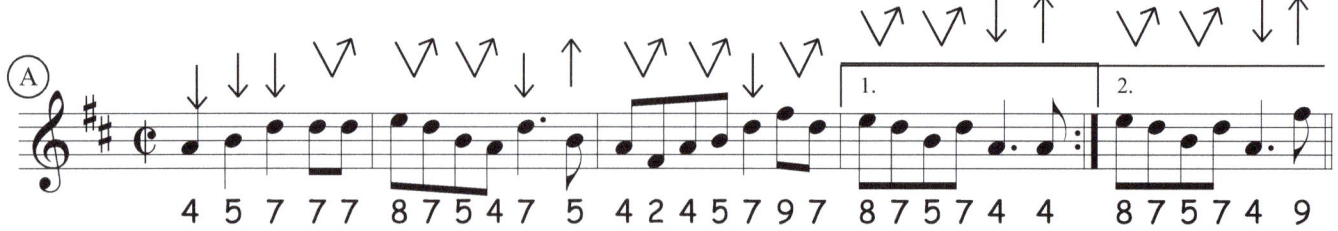

4 5 7 7 7 8 7 5 4 7 5 4 2 4 5 7 9 7 8 7 5 7 4 4   8 7 5 7 4 9

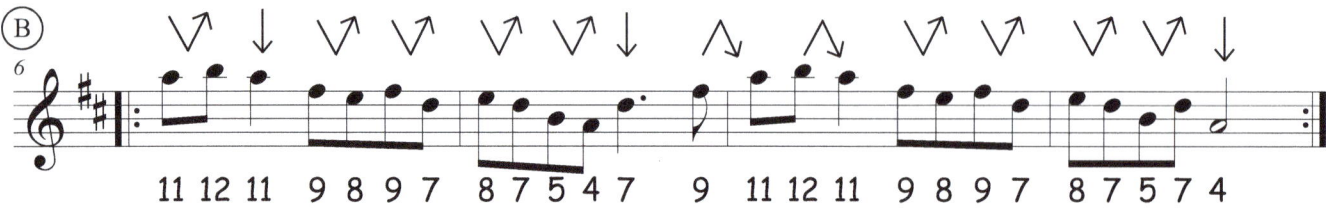

11 12 11 9 8 9 7 8 7 5 4 7 9 11 12 11 9 8 9 7 8 7 5 7 4

Source: Luther Davis (1887-1986) Galax, Virginia

Chord Chart

A Part	D	D	D	A D
Part B	D	D	D	A D

This tune is easy to learn because it uses the D pentatonic scale which omits the fourth and seventh tones of the scale: D E F# G A B C# D. There are no Gs or C#s.

Short lyric as sung by Luther:

> They had a little dance
> on the upper end of town.
> They didn't ask me
> or Cousin Sally Brown.

Here is Luther Davis, age 90, sitting in front of the heating stove in his home. Jim and I learned this tune from Luther in 1979. For at least eight years, we spent one Saturday a month playing tunes, eating, and talking in his home.

DOWN BY THE SALLEY GARDENS

Key: D
Tuning: dddd or DAd

Traditional Irish Aire:
"The Maids of Mourne Shore"

Chord Chart

D	G D	G A	D
D	G D	G A	D
Bm	A	G A	D
D	G D	G A	D

Let's slow down and play something beautiful. Many years ago I learned this song in an Irish session. It reminded me of *Down by the Willow Garden*, an Appalachian murder ballad in which the young man kills the one he "loves" three different ways! I had often heard that song, also called *Rose Connelly*, at Virginia fiddlers conventions in Grayson and Carroll County. The first recorded version was by famous local musicians G. B. Grayson and Henry Whitter, hence the popularity. I choose to sing the beautiful lyrics written in 1889 by William Butler Yeats. The song, *The Rambling Boys of Pleasure*, had been published in Ireland the year before. Yeats seems to have borrowed a few lines of it for his poem. Coincidentally, a salley garden is a grove of willow trees.

Down by the Salley Gardens

William Butler Yeats

Down by the salley gardens
　my love and I did meet;
She passed the salley gardens
　with little snow-white feet.
She bid me take love easy,
　as the leaves grow on the tree;
But I, being young and foolish,
　with her would not agree.

In a field down by the river
　my love and I did stand,
And on my leaning shoulder
　she laid her snow-white hand.
She bid me take life easy,
　as the grass grows on the weirs;
But I was young and foolish,
　and now am full of tears.

D Tunes

THE EIGHTH OF JANUARY

Key: D
Tuning: dddd or DAd

Traditional

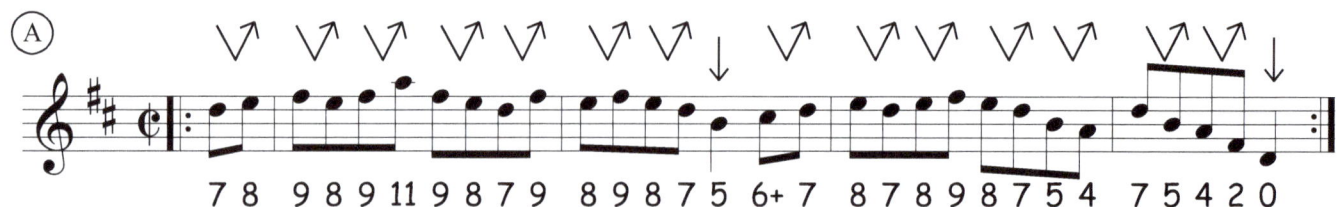

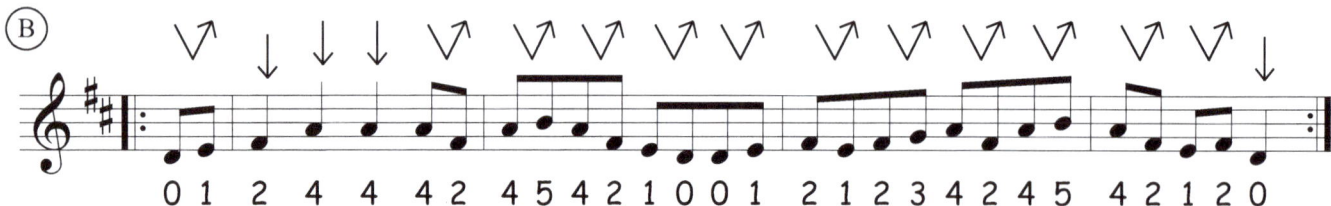

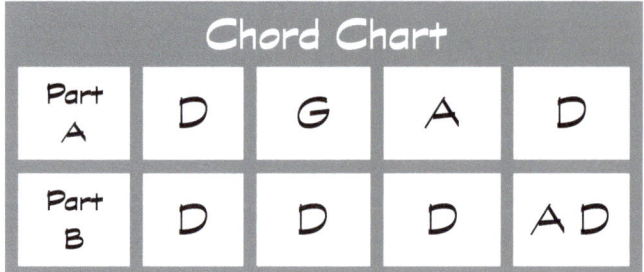

On January 8, 1815, General Andrew Jackson led a small, ill-equipped army against a large British force of over 8,000 battle hardened troops. Jackson and the battle became immediately famous and a source of national pride. A tune was created and circulated commemorating the event known as the *Eighth of January* or *Jackson's Victory*.

A highly regarded school teacher/musician/poet named James Morris, aka Jimmy Driftwood, lived and worked in an area rich in musical tradition. He developed a fun teaching strategy of taking historical events and expressing them in poetic/lyric form and setting them to tunes with which his students were familiar. This was Driftwood's most famous song recorded by him around 1958 as *The Battle of New Orleans*. In 1959 the famous country singer, Johnny Horton, recorded the song and it became a top "hit" on the Billboard charts. It remains quite popular and widely known to this very day.

While on our camping trip to California we pulled into Mountain View, Arkansas, on June 20, 1987. By a fortunate turn of events, we were met by a group of street session musicians. We struck up a conversation and were invited to attend that evening's community celebration of Jimmy Driftwood's 80th birthday. Jim and I were blessed to sit and visit with Jimmy Driftwood at this wonderful community party serving homemade pot-luck food and traditional cakes made by regular folks in that mountain community. As we sat chatting with Jimmy about our common interests, we ended up doing what school teachers always do. We talked shop.

The musical bow, string bow, or bowstring is a simple string instrument which came to America via the slave trade. Made of a flexible wooden stick strung end to end with a taut cord (pig gut, perhaps) or metal string, it is a type of jaw harp held against the teeth/jaw, and as the string is plucked, the mouth resonates the sound. Jimmy could actually play tunes on this instrument!

D Tunes

GRASSHOPPER SITTIN' ON A SWEET POTATO VINE

Key: D
Tuning: dddd or DAd

Traditional

A

4 5 4 3 2 3 4 7 9 11 9 8 7 7 4 5 7 5 4 3 4 5 7 5 4 4 5

4 5 4 3 2 4 7 8 9 11 9 8 7 7 5 6+ 7 6+ 5 4 5 6+ 4 7 8 7

B

8 9 8 7 6+ 7 8 9 11 9 8 7 7 4 5 7 5 4 3 4 5 7 5 4 4 7

8 9 8 7 6+ 7 8 9 11 9 8 7 7 5 6+ 7 6+ 5 4 5 6+ 4 7 8 7

Source: Luther Davis, (1887-1986) Galax, VA

Chord Chart

Part A	D	D	G	G D
	D	D	A	D
Part B	A	D	G	G D
	A	D	A	D

Traditional fiddlers would occasionally take modern and popular tunes and doctor them a bit to turn them into excellent, two-part dance tunes. If you listen carefully to this tune, you will hear *The Battle Hymn of the Republic* clothed in fiddle garb.

Lyrics

Grasshopper sittin' on a sweet potato vine, (3X),
Along came a chicken and says, "He's mine."

LIFTING FOG

Key: D
Tuning: dddd or DAd

Phyllis Gaskins

Chord Chart

Part A	D	D	G	G	D	A7	D	D
	D	D7	G	G	D	A7	D	D
Part B	G	G	D	D	G	G	A7	A7
	D	D7	G	G	D	A7	D	D

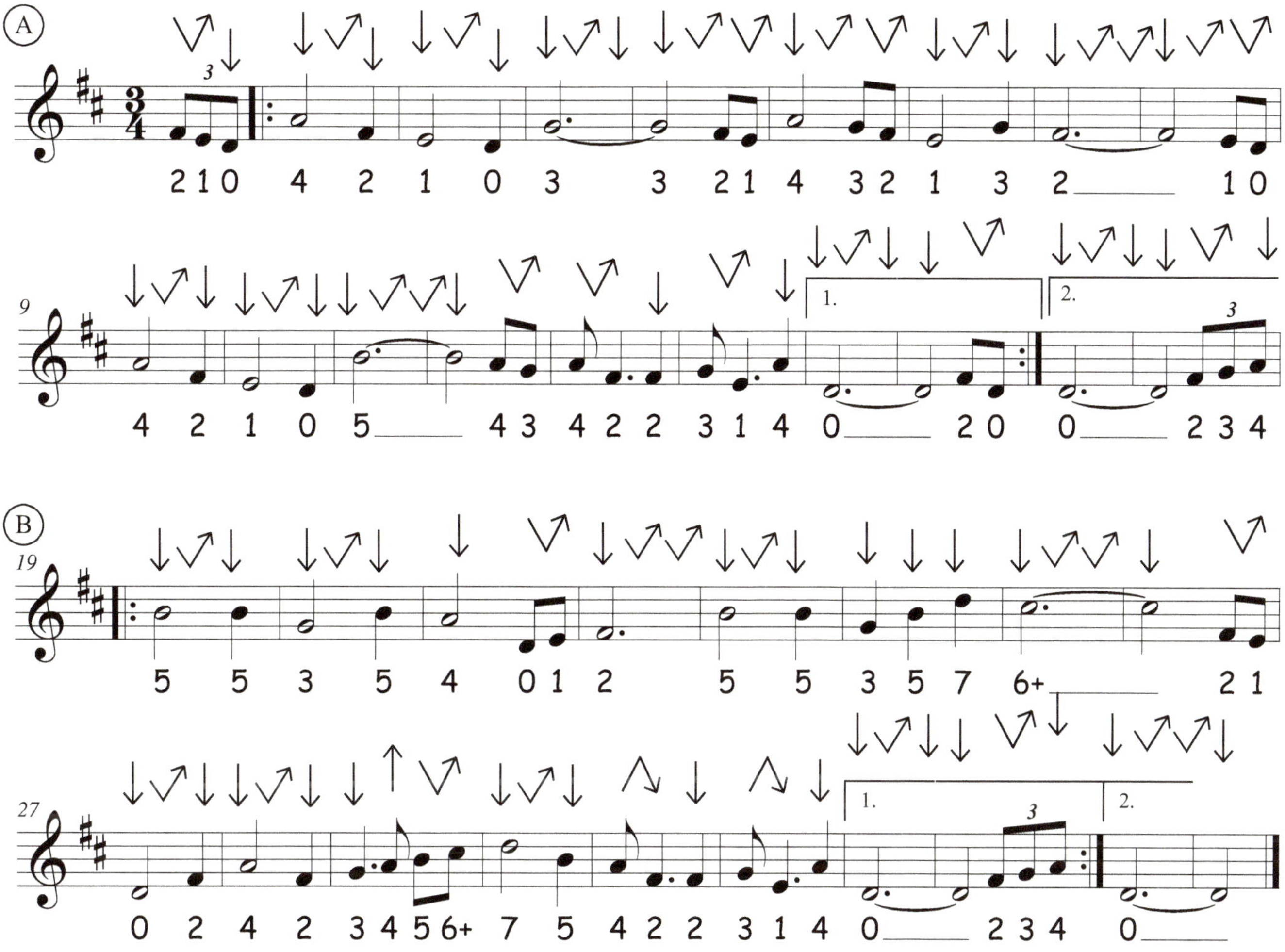

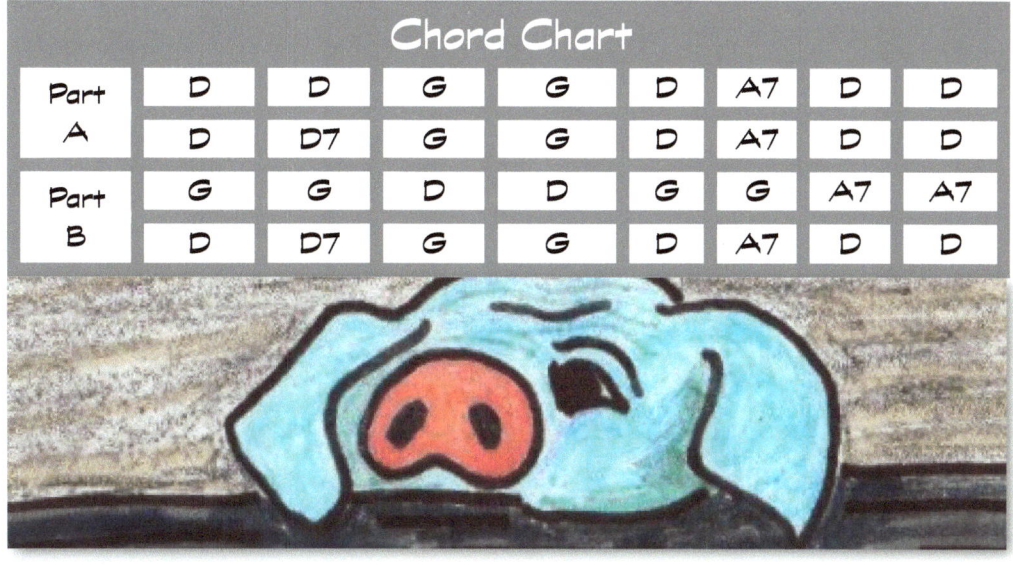

As I was washing dishes, the kitchen window view was all ground fog so thick I could not see anything but gray. Then the fog lifted, slowly showing a straight line dividing the ground from the fog as if someone were raising a curtain before the play of day.

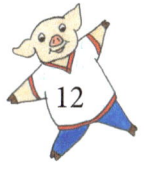

D Tunes

LILY OF THE VALLEY

Key: D
Tuning: dddd or DAd

Traditional

A

7 5 4 5 7 7 8 7 5 7 8 9 8 9 8 7 4 5 4 5 7 8 9 8 7 5 7 5 7 5

4 5 7 7 8 7 5 7 8 9 8 9 8 7 4 5 4 5 7 8 9 8 6+ 7 8 7

B

11 11 9 8 7 8 9 8 7 7 8 9 10 9 11 11 9 8 7 8 9 8 7 8 5 7 5 11 11

9 8 7 8 9 8 7 7 8 9 8 9 8 7 4 5 4 5 7 8 9 8 6+ 7 8 7

Source: Luther Davis, (1887-1986) Galax, Virginia

Chord Chart

Part A	D	D	D	Bm
	D	D	D A	D
Part B	D	D	D	Bm
	D	D	D A	D

Visiting Luther Davis in his Galax home to learn tunes, hear his stories, and eat a lunch of beans and biscuits was a favorite monthly adventure for Jim and me. We would listen and watch. We would play a tune, then Luther would say, "You've not got that quite right." We would watch and listen again and again. We were not "quick studies," learning to play the instruments and the tunes at the same time. He was patient and forgiving. Once when we thought we had learned all of the tunes that he knew, he met us at the screen door saying, "I thought of another tune. It's not much of a tune, but we'll play it anyway. Isom and Fielden liked it. It's called *Lily of the Valley*. To our surprise it wasn't the hymn we knew by the same name.

MORPETH RANT

D Tunes

Key: D
Tuning: dddd or DAd

Traditional

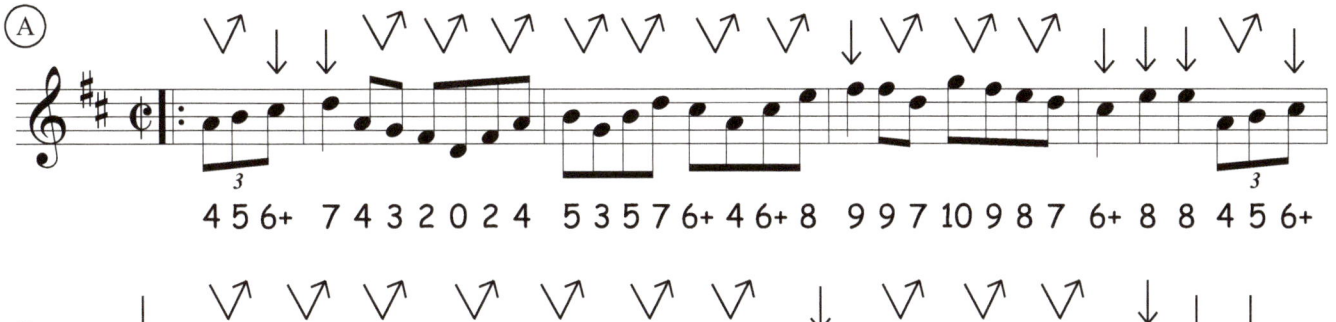

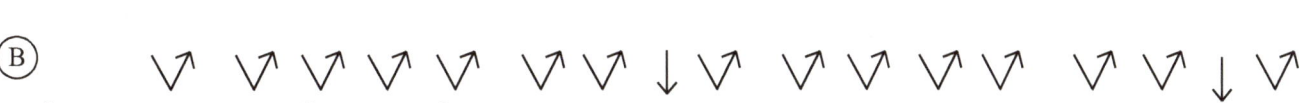

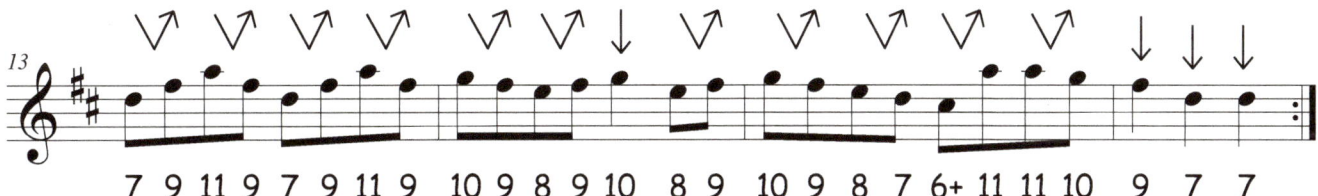

Chord Chart				
Part A	D	G A	D G	A
	D	G A	D G	A D
Part B	D	G	A	D
	D	G	A	D

A few decades ago we learned this tune from our friend, Tom Walsh in an Old Time session at a fiddlers' convention somewhere in Southwest Virginia. Much later we learned the tune comes from Morpeth, Northumberland County, England, and was a Morris Dance in 2/4 time which morphed into 4/4 time and square dance tempo as so many "borrowed" tunes were.

NANCY BLEVINS

Key: D
Tuning: dddd or DAd

Traditional

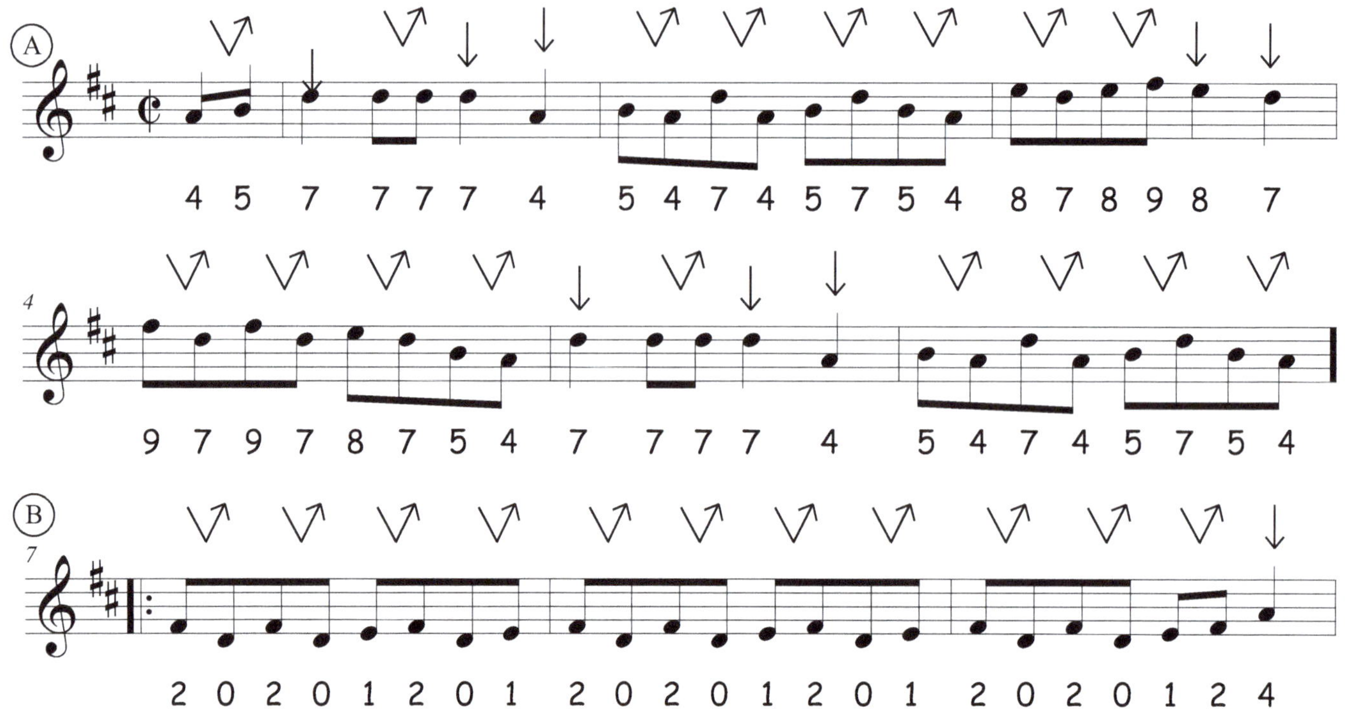
A
4 5 7 7 7 7 4 5 4 7 4 5 7 5 4 8 7 8 9 8 7
4
9 7 9 7 8 7 5 4 7 7 7 7 4 5 4 7 4 5 7 5 4
B
7
2 0 2 0 1 2 0 1 2 0 2 0 1 2 0 1 2 0 2 0 1 2 4

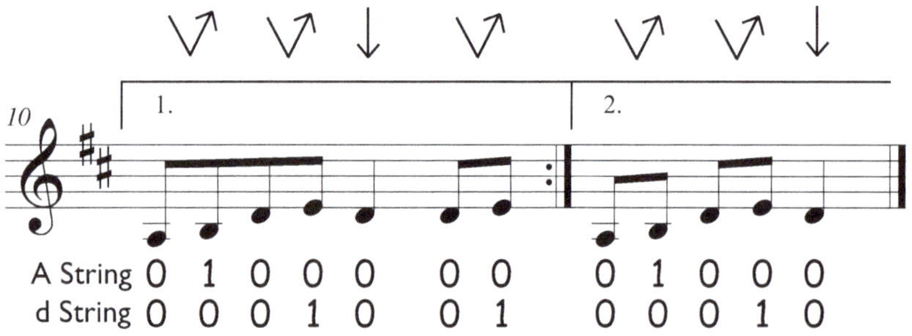
10
1.
2.
A String 0 1 0 0 0 0 0 0 1 0 0 0
d String 0 0 0 1 0 0 1 0 0 0 1 0

Chord Chart

Part A	D	D	A7
	A7	D	D
Part B	D	D	D
	A7 D		

Source: Albert Hash (1917-1983) Grayson County, VA

Help Note: The first and second endings have a low A and a low B which are not possible on the Galax dulcimer. I just play the open d and let the fiddle carry those low notes. If your dulcimer is tuned DAd, then you can get those two low notes on the middle string by using the open A string and fretting the first fret of the middle string for the low B.

Albert Hash, a friend to all and a "fixture" at the Independence Fiddlers' Convention, is pictured here playing a fiddle that he made.

Nancy Blevins, a cousin of Albert Hash's grandfather, may have written this tune.

FIDDLERS CONVENTION
INDEPENDENCE BALL PARK — Independence, Virginia
FRIDAY, JUNE 24, 1983 — 5:00 P.M.
SATURDAY, JUNE 25, 1983 — 4:00 P.M.
ALBERT HASH

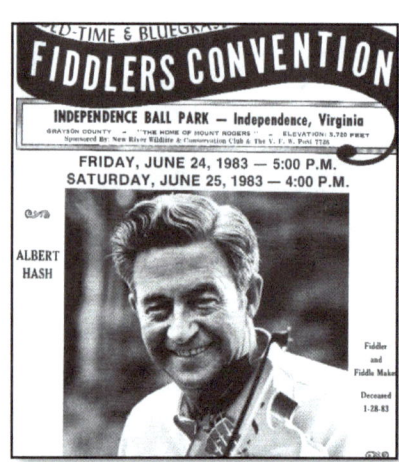

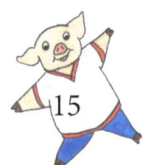

D Tunes

NEEDLECASE

Key: D
Tuning: dddd or DAd

Traditional

(A) 11 10 9 8 7 5 10 5 10 11 10 9 8 7 5 4 5 6+ 4 8

11 10 9 8 7 5 10 5 10 4 6+ 8 6+ 5 4 5 4 5 6+ 7

(B) 0 2 4 7 5 5 4 5 7 0 2 4 7 5 4 5 6+ 4 4

0 2 4 7 5 5 4 5 7 4 6+ 8 6+ 5 4 5 4 5 6+ 7

Chord Chart				
Part A	D	G	D	A D
	D	G	A	A D
Part B	D	G	D	A D
	D	G	A	A D

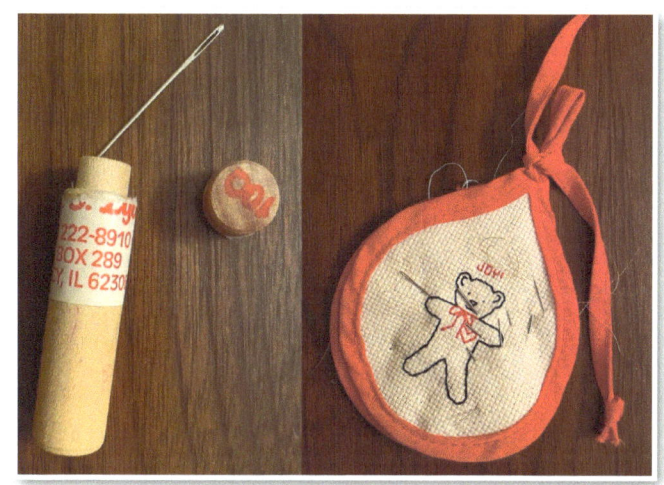

Lori's Needlecases
Photos by Lori Lineweaver

When I was a small child, Grandma had two wooden needlecases much like the one in the left photo. She kept the small needles in one and the larger needles in the other one. She always had me do the threading of the needles with the small eyes because "young eyes can see better than old eyes."

ROCKING MY BABIES TO SLEEP

Key: D
Tune: dddd or DAd

Traditional

*4 The fret number is for dddd tuned dulcimers. If you are tuned to DAd, then you need to use the fret/finger placement for the DAd tuning. Low A is the melody note which I do not have on my Galax dulcimer. If you're in DAd, play the open A string.

**1 The melody note is C# which can be found in DAd tuning on the second fret of the second string. My Galax does not have this note. I play the 1st fret, first string which gives me an e.

D Tunes

Chord Chart

Part A	D	A7	D	D
	A7	A7	D	D
	D	A7	D	D
	A7	A7	D	D
Part B	D	G	D	D
	A7	A7	D	D
	D	G	D	D
	A7	A7	D	D

The Old Time music community owes a debt of gratitude to musician and folklorist Alan Jabbour (1942-2017) who did the field recordings of Henry Reed and his family. Alan Jabbour's band, The Hollow Rock String Band, recorded a number of these in the early 1970s which became standard jam session tunes at fiddler conventions all over the USA. Alan later became the founding director of the American Folklife Center at the Library of Congress.

Jim and I attended the 17th Annual Henry Reed Memorial Fiddlers Convention, June 14-15, 2019 at the Newport Community Center in Newport, Virginia. We had gone a few days early to catch up with friends we had not seen in two years. One of those was Dean Reed, son of Henry Reed. He came to our campsite early in the morning on Friday as we were having breakfast. He knocked at the door and said to Jim, "Come on out and play that *Rocking My Babies to Sleep* for me." Of course we did! It had been two years, and he remembered Jim playing that tune for him.

D Tunes

ROCK THAT CRADLE, JOE

Key: D
Tuning: dddd or DAd

Traditional

A

9 10 | 11 11 11 9 | 9 10 11 | 11 11 9 | 9 10 11 | 11 11 9 8 7 | 9 | 7 8

9 8 7 | 7 8 9 | 8 7 | 8 9 10 | 9 8 7 6+ | 7 | 9 10 | 7 | 6+ 5

B

4 6+ 8 | 6+ 6+ 7 | 8 9 | 8 9 10 | 9 10 11 9 | 10 9 | 6+ 5

4 6+ 8 | 6+ 6+ 7 | 8 9 | 8 9 10 | 9 8 7 6+ | 7 | 6+ 5 | 7

Lyrics (Sing verse on second A Part and chorus on the first B Part.)

1. Gotta go home, gotta go to bed,
Gotta get up in the morning.
What we gonna do if the baby cries?
Rock that cradle, Joe.

Chorus
Rock that cradle, rock the cradle,
Rock that cradle, Joe,
Rock that cradle, rock the cradle,
Rock it nice and slow.

2. Gotta go to bed, gotta go to sleep,
Gotta go to work in the morning,
What we gonna do if the baby cries?
Rock that cradle, Joe.
Chorus

3. What we gonna do if the baby cries,
I do not know,
What we gonna do if the baby cries?
Rock that cradle, Joe.
Chorus

Chord Chart				
Part A	D	D	D	D
	D	D	A	D
Part B	A	D	G	D
	A	D	A	D

D Tunes

TRUDE EVANS

Key: D
Tuning: dddd or DAd

Traditional

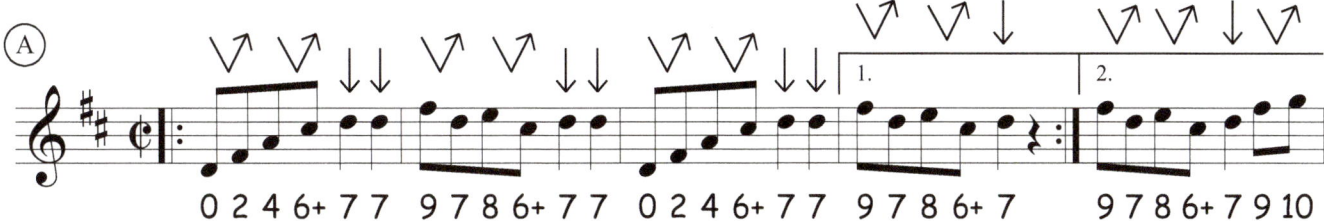

0 2 4 6+ 7 7   9 7 8 6+ 7 7   0 2 4 6+ 7 7   9 7 8 6+ 7   9 7 8 6+ 7 9 10

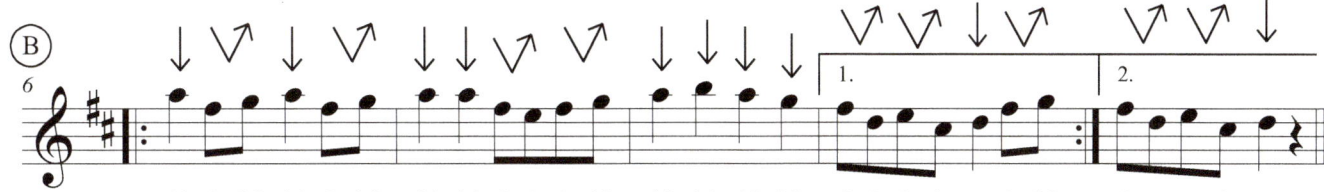

11 9 10 11 9 10   11 11 9 8 9 10   11 12 11 10   9 7 8 6+ 7 9 10   9 7 8 6+ 7

In my first book I included two different variants of *Walking in the Parlor*. *Trude Evans* is another version gleaned from the playing of West Virginia fiddler, French Carpenter. He is said to have learned it from a lady named Trude Evans. Researchers of Old Time tunes identify *Walking in the Parlor/Trude Evans* as Appalachian variants of the English tune *Shepherd's Hey*. One sometimes wonders about the evolution of tunes passed from one fiddler to another. Tunes traveled from the Old Country, across the ocean on ships, to the New World's plantations, cabins, and towns. Tunes survived aurally for generations and ended up being transcribed, recorded, and played in sessions all over the country. It is easy to understand how tunes morph and lose their original names or keep names while changing the melodies a little or entirely!

Chord Chart

Part A	D	D	D	A D
	D	D	D	A D
Part B	D	D	D	A D
	D	D	D	A D

D Tunes

TUCKER'S BARN

Key: D
Tuning: dddd or DAd

Traditional

Ⓐ

4 6+ 7 9 7 4 6+ 8 6+ 7 8 9 7 6+ 4 6+ 7 8 9 10 8 8 7 5 4 5 3 3 4 6+

7 9 7 4 6+ 8 6+ 7 8 9 7 6+ 4 6+ 7 8 9 10 8 8 7 5 4 5 3 3 8 9

Ⓑ

10 11 10 8 7 5 4 3 4 5 3 1 0 1 2 3 4 5 7 5 4 3 2 3 4 2 0 0 1

2 4 2 4 6 5 4 3 4 5 3 1 0 1 2 3 4 5 7 5 4 3 2 3 4 2 0 0 1

2 4 2 4 6 5 4 3 4 5 3 1 0 1 2 3 4 5 7 5 4 3 2 3 4 2 0

Source: Gaither Wiley Carlton (1901 – 1972), Wilkes County, North Carolina

Chord Chart

Part A	D	D	D	*D	G
	D	D	D	*D	G
Part B	G	G Em	G	D	
	D	G Em	G	D	
	D	G Em	G	D	

*D 2/4 measures

21

Tucker's Barn Community

Early American communities were often named after local landmarks such as stores, courthouses, churches, lakes, taverns, etc. Tucker's Barn was the community gathering place for meetings, dances, parties, and other community activities. It became the center of a thriving community and an important local town. When Caldwell County, North Carolina, needed a county seat and courthouse, Tucker's Barn was the logical choice. County leaders, however, decided a county seat named Tucker's Barn would seem strange and archaic. So they renamed the town Lenoir after the local Revolutionary War hero General William Lenoir.

In 1976 the USA celebrated its 200th birthday. Traditional square and round dancing experienced a revival along with Old Time Appalachian music. There were many local barn dances and frolics in our area of Virginia, and we, The Elk Run String Band, enjoyed playing for them. Alas! *Tucker's Barn* is only good for flatfoot or buck dancing.

Karen Lee, Phyllis, Jim, Bill Trapp, Mel Lee

What's a Crooked Tune?

Most traditional dance tunes are easy to learn because of the predictable pattern of two eight-measure parts, A and B. Each is repeated, giving a total of 32 measures for the dances. Those 32 measures are cycled repeatedly throughout the duration of the dance. *Tucker's Barn* is a crooked tune, which means it has an uneven count. Some crooked tunes drop or add beats or even entire measures. Some have a short part and a long part. This makes them a wee bit more difficult to learn and also impossible to use for square and round dances. You will notice that for the A Part, *Tucker's Barn* has a first line of three 4/4 measures and one 2/4 measure. Then it goes back to 4/4. This repeats in the second line. The B Part has 12 measures. Yes, that's correct!

Watch out! There are more crooked tunes in this book. They will not, however, have the same complicated structure as *Tucker's Barn*.

D Tunes

TWIN SISTERS

Key: D
Tuning: dddd or DAd

Traditional

A) 7 5 4 2 0 2 4 4 5___ 4 5 7 8 7 8 9 11 9 8 9 8 7 9 8 7 5 7 5

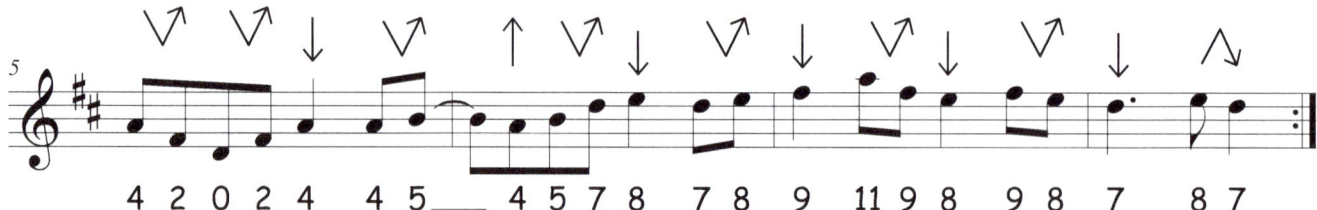

4 2 0 2 4 4 5___ 4 5 7 8 7 8 9 11 9 8 9 8 7 8 7

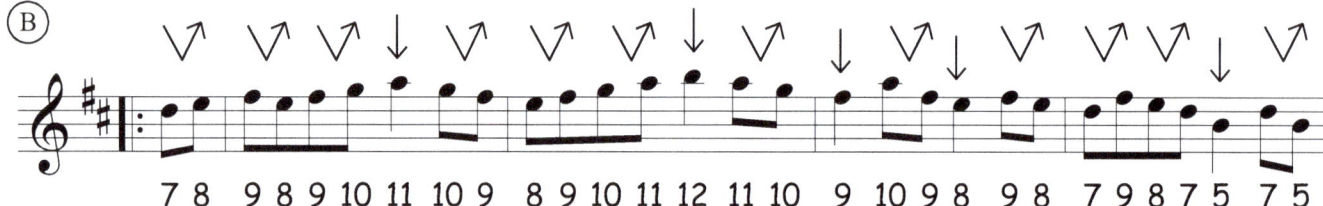

B) 7 8 9 8 9 10 11 10 9 8 9 10 11 12 11 10 9 10 9 8 9 8 7 9 8 7 5 7 5

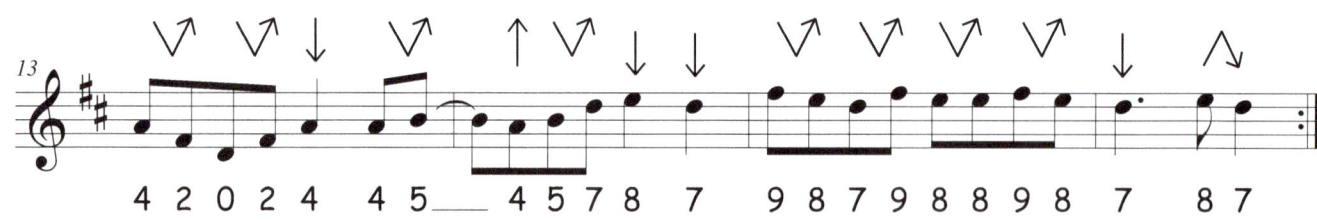

4 2 0 2 4 4 5___ 4 5 7 8 7 9 8 7 9 8 8 9 8 7 8 7

Chord Chart

A Part	D	G	D A	D G
	D	G	A	D
B Part	D	G	D A	D G
	D	G	A	D

Twin Sisters is a Franklin County, Virginia, tune published in 1839 as the *Two Sisters* in the first collection of American fiddle tunes, *George P. Knauff's Virginia Reels*. Knauff was from Farmville, Virginia. Another popular version at fiddle festivals comes mainly from the playing of West Virginia fiddler Melvin Wine. This tune is an American variant of the Irish hornpipe, *The Boys of Bluehill*.

G TUNES

ME: "Hi, folks! Mind if I join ya in a few tunes?"

ENOCH RUTHERFORD: "Naw! Pull up a cha'r and git that delcimore tuned for G tunes!"

ME: "I don't need to retune. I'm ready! Let's play!"

I love playing G Tunes on my Galax Dulcimer because they sit in just the right place on the fretboard. Before the 6.5 fret was added to the fretboard, the Ionian scale started on the third fret.

G Tunes almost always use the G major scale: G A B C D E F# G
                                              3 4 5 6 7 8 9   10

The G major (Ionian) scale starts on fret #3 in all of the tunings used in the G Tunes section of this book:

1. **dddd** (Galax tuning)

2. **Dddd** (Bagpipe tuning)

3. **DGd** (This is called reverse Ionian tuning by many folks because the traditional tuning for G is GDd. In the early 1970s the tuning of the bass and middle strings swapped tones.)

QUESTION: So, Ms. Phyllis, are some of these tunes missing some of the tones of the G major scale?

ANSWER: Yes. Several tunes are missing one or two notes, and these are referred to as gapped scale tunes in Old Time music. There is a special gapped scale called the pentatonic scale. It always leaves out the 4th and 7th tones of the scale. In the G scale the missing tones would be C and F#. *Mulvahill's Polkas* are written using gapped scales.

G Tunes

BARLOW KNIFE

Key: G
Tune: dddd or DGd

Traditional

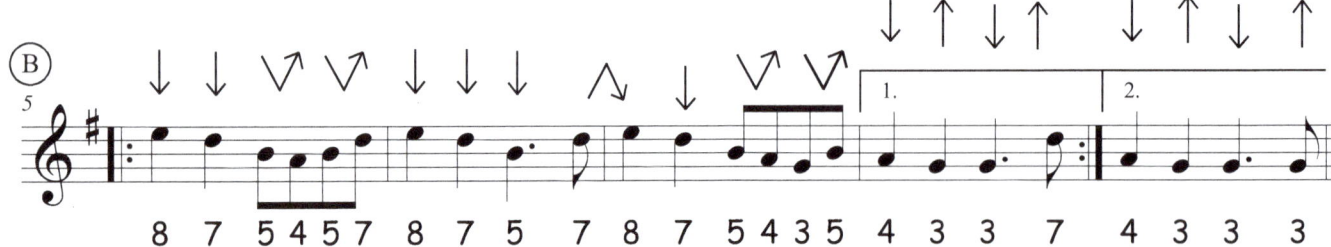
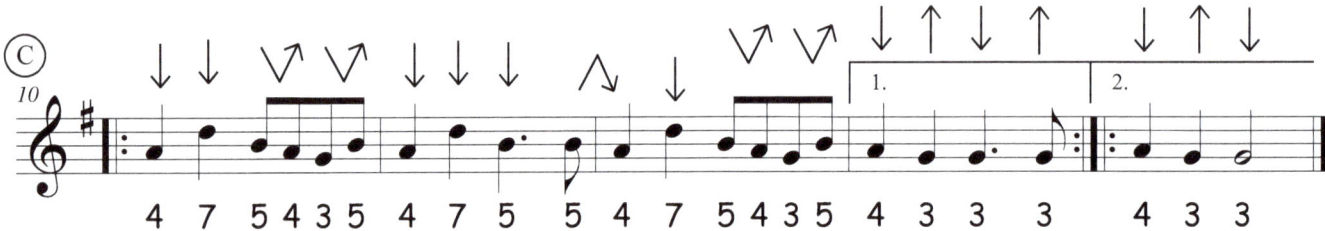

A Part	G	G	G	G
B Part	G	G	G	D G
C Part	D	D	D	D G

Chord Chart

Lyrics

A Part
I've been workin' all my life
All I've got is a Barlow knife.

B Part
Buckhorn handle and a Barlow blade.
Best durn knife that ever was made.

C Part
Take my dog, take my wife,
   Please don't take my Barlow knife.

Versions of *Barlow Knife* have been found throughout the upper South and Mississippi. Our version, learned at fiddlers' convention jam sessions, is most similar to the one collected by Alan Jabbour from Virginia fiddler Henry Reed. This tune honors a beloved knife important in the lives of early Americans and their descendants since the 18th century. The Barlow Knife design originated in England around 1670. Obadiah Barlow was the first entrepreneur to manufacture them. In 1745, his grandson John started the exportation of these knives to America where they became an expensive, highly valued "necessity" useful for many workaday activities.

ME: "So, Brent. Tell me all about your Barlow Knife."

BRENT: "My Barlow knife has an Imperial blade made in Ireland and a buckhorn handle. I purchased it at the hardware store in Bridgewater in the '70s; it still lives on my worktable for odd jobs and handy work."

BILLY IN THE LOWLAND

G Tunes

Key: G
Tuning: dddd or DGd

Traditional

A

0 3 4 3 4 5 7 8 7 5 7 8 7 5 4 3 5 4 3 1 3 1 0 2

3 4 3 4 5 7 10 11 12 10 11 10 8 9 10 9 8 7 5 3 0 2 3

B

8 9 10 11 12 11 10 10 7 8 7 5 7 8 7 5 4 3 4 3 1 3 1 0

10 11 12 11 10 10 7 7 8 7 5 7 8 9 10 9 8 7 5 3 0 2 3

Source: Henry Reed, (1894 -1969), Glen Lyn, Virginia

Chord Chart

A Part	G	G	G	D
	G	G	C D	G
B Part	G	G	Am	D
	G	G	C Am	D G

Alan Jabbour (1942-2017)

Billy in the Lowland is another tune that became popular at fiddler's conventions during the early 1970s thanks to Alan Jabbour and The Hollow Rock String Band. Jabbour started recording the music of Henry Reed when Reed was in his 80s. Jabbour taught the old tunes to musicians eager to learn them. Jabbour's collective work, *Fiddle Tunes of the Old Frontier: The Henry Reed Collection*, is massive. His transcribed tunes, collection of family photos, and interviews with the Reed family can be accessed through the Library of Congress website.

G Tunes

COTTON-EYED JOE

Key: G
Tuning: dddd or DGd

Traditional

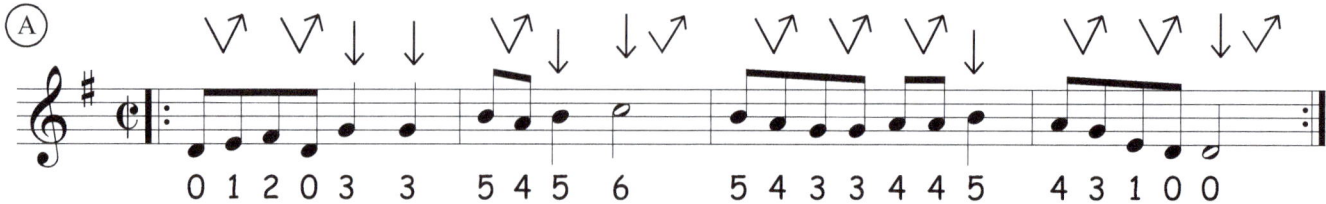

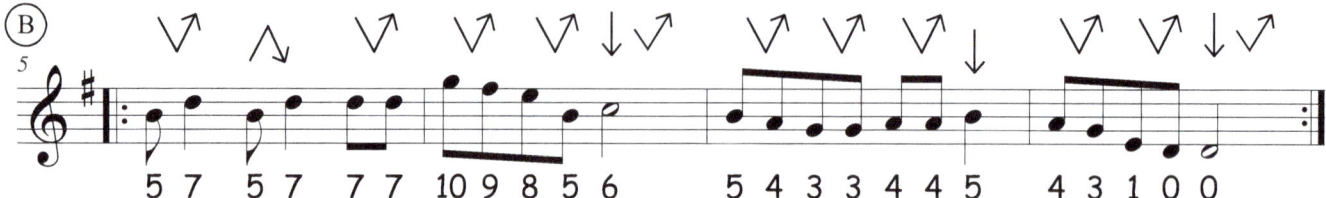

Chord Chart

A Part	G	G C	G	D G
B Part	G	G C	G	D G

Lyrics

A Part

1. Way back yonder, long time ago,
   Daddy worked a man called
   Cotton-Eyed Joe.

B Part Refrain

   Where did you come from,
   where did you go?
   Where did you come from,
   Cotton-Eyed Joe?

2. I'd been married a long time ago,
   If it hadn't been for
   Cotton-Eyed Joe.

Refrain

3. Old bull fiddle and shoe-string bow,
   Wouldn't play nothin' but
   Cotton-Eyed Joe.

Refrain

WHERE DID "COTTON-EYED JOE" COME FROM?

Cotton-Eyed Joe is a traditional folk song, fiddle tune, and dance widespread throughout the U.S. and Canada. It originated in the American south prior to the Civil War and was a popular song of the workers on the plantations. When I play this tune, I think of the toils and sadness of the enslaved people and how they were able to persevere through it all. A Nameless One managed to play the fiddle and compose this tune. It has remained extremely popular to this day in its many variants. We need to honor the creativity of all the people who have contributed so much to our native folk music.

It is believed that "cotton-eyed" is an ailment of the eyes caused by some known or unknown bacterial infection which turns the eyes milky white. I remember a distant cousin who was cotton-eyed. He worked odd jobs on people's farms and stayed in barns and sheds wherever he worked. My parents never let me get close to him, but Dad helped him as most of the people in our poor dirt-farming community did. Daddy said it was the Christian thing to do.

GENTLE MAIDEN (AN MAIGDEAN CEANNSA)

Key: G
Tuning: dddd or DGd

Traditional - Irish

G Tunes

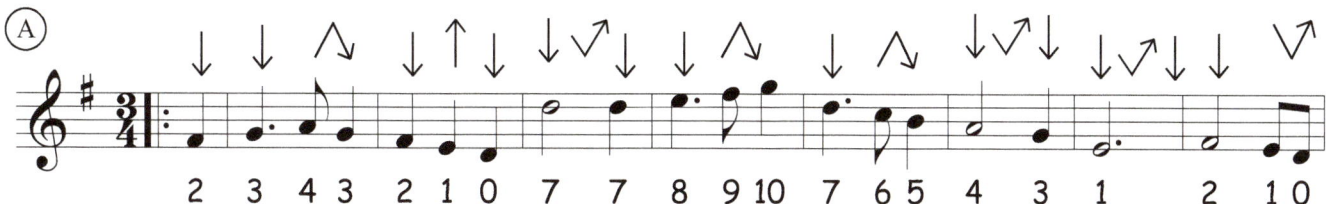

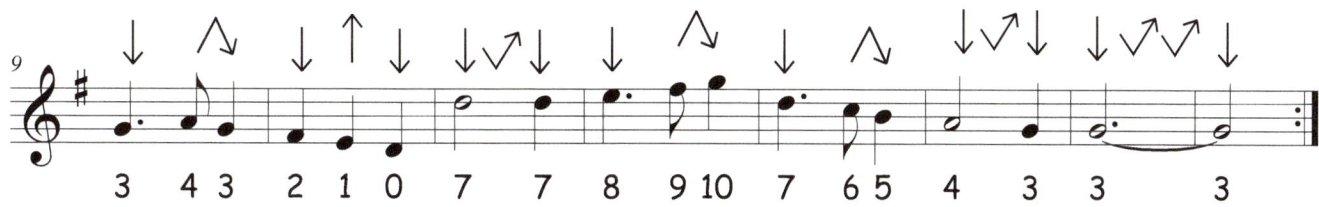

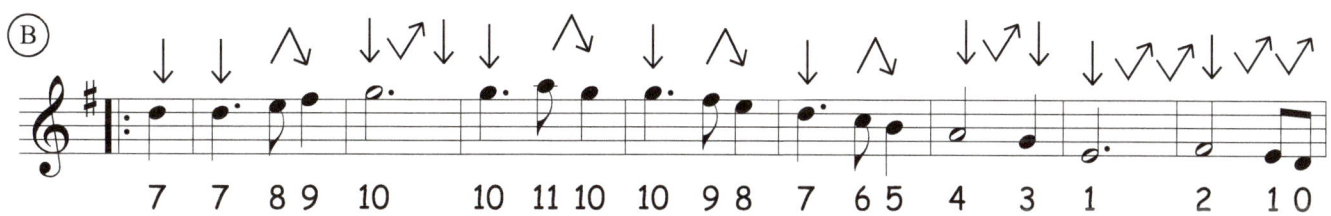

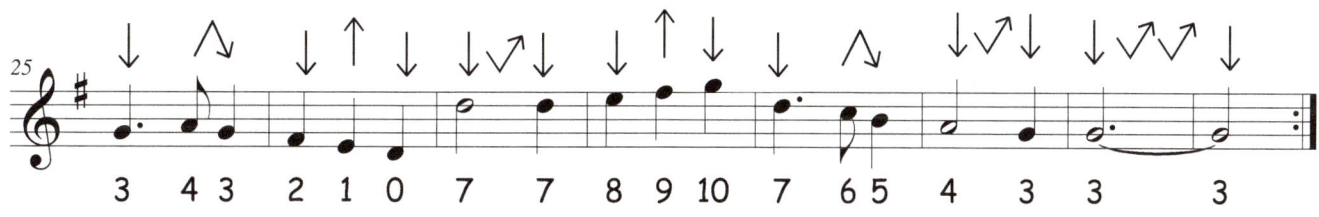

This Irish air *An Maigdean Ceannsa* (also known as *When the South Wind Blows*) is thought to be a symbolic reference to Ireland. Sir Harold Boulton (England, 1859-1935) wrote the beautiful lyrics which were translated by the first president of Ireland, Douglas Hyde (1860-1949). It was first recorded in 1940 by the great Irish tenor John McCormack.

G Tunes

THE IRISH WASHERWOMAN

Key: G
Tuning: dddd or DGd

Traditional Irish Jig

During the 1970s and '80s, Jim and I would camp out in downtown Independence, Virginia, on the high school athletics field for the annual fiddler's convention. Mr. James Stamper lived in Independence and every year he would seek us out to play the *Irish Washerwoman* for him. Each time he would tell us that no one in the area played it anymore.

It is one of two rare jigs from the old country that survived in the Grayson/Carroll County area until the present day. The other jig is *Chapel Hill March*, reshaped into a reel called *Green Willis*, most likely by the great Carroll County fiddler Taylor Kimble. Both of these tunes can be found in my first Galax Dulcimer book, *Galax Dulcimer - Job of Journey Work*.

Chord Chart

Part A	G	G	D	D
	G	G	D	G
Part B	G	G	D	D
	C G	C G	C D	G

JAMIE ALLEN

Key: G
Tuning: dddd or DGd

Traditional

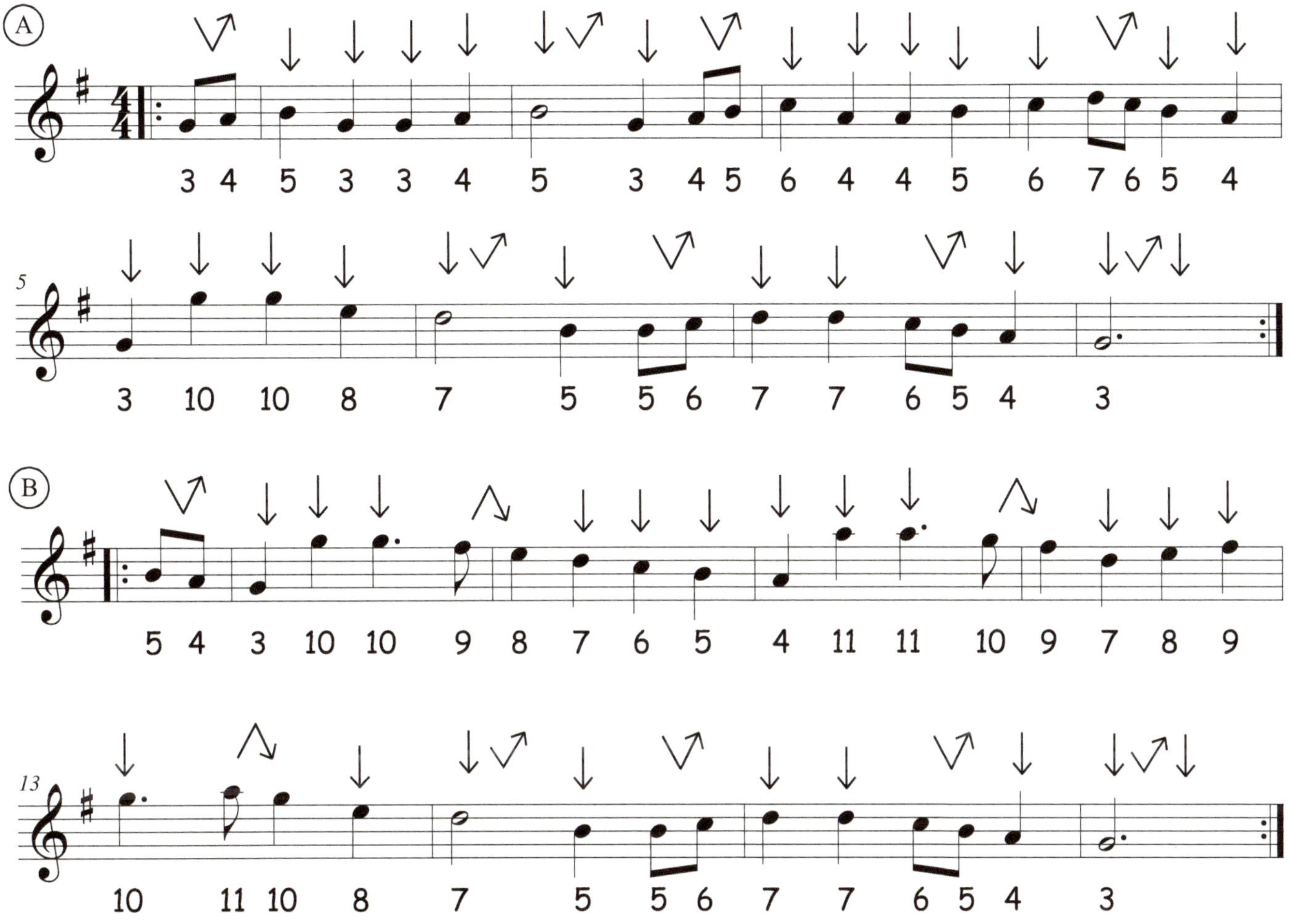

Chord Chart

Part A	G	G	D	D
	G	G	D	G
Part B	G	G	D	D
	G	G	D	G

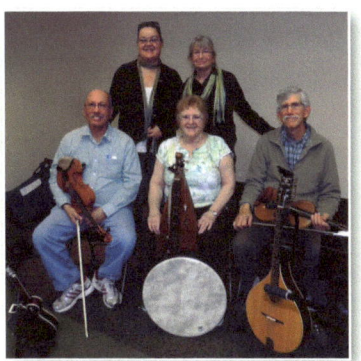

The Old Favorites, 2017
Back row:
Cheryl Tobler, Rae Kasdan
Front row:
Jim Gaskins, Phyllis Gaskins, Steve Kasdan
Photo by Manuel Jose
Thanks, Manny!

Members of The Old Favorites Band and other wonderful friends gather in Bridgewater, Virginia, for Sunday afternoon Irish sessions. One of my favorite session tunes is *Jamie Allen*, a Northumbrian rant, which can be easily added to a polka set. Jamie Allen (c. 1734-1810) was a celebrated smallpipes player well-known as "the duke's piper" in Northumbria. He was a notorious character in England who was convicted of horse-stealing and died in prison.

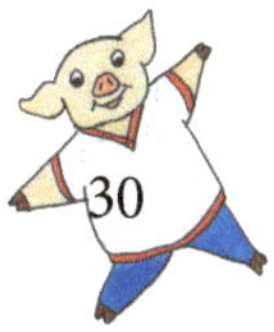

G Tunes

LOST GIRL

Key: G
Tuning: dddd or DGd

Traditional

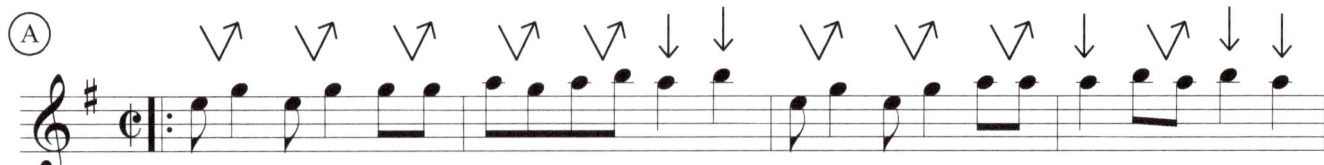

8 10 8 10 10 10 11 10 11 12 11 12   8 10 8 10 11 11 11 12 11 12 11

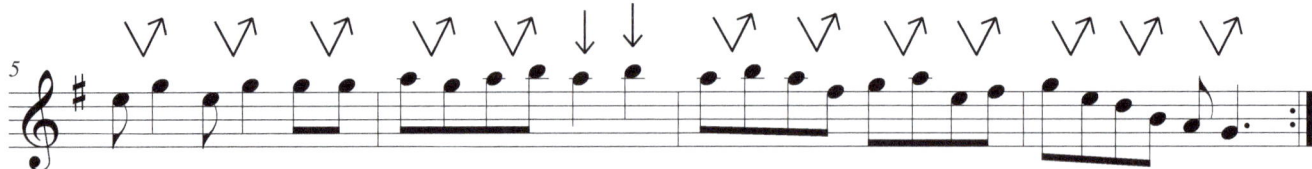

8 10 8 10 10 10 11 10 11 12 11 12   11 12 11 9 10 11 8 9 10 8 7 5 4 3

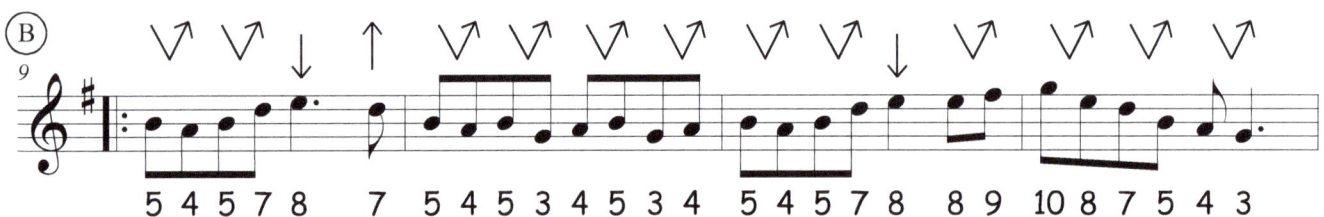

5 4 5 7 8   7   5 4 5 3 4 5 3 4   5 4 5 7 8   8 9 10 8 7 5 4 3

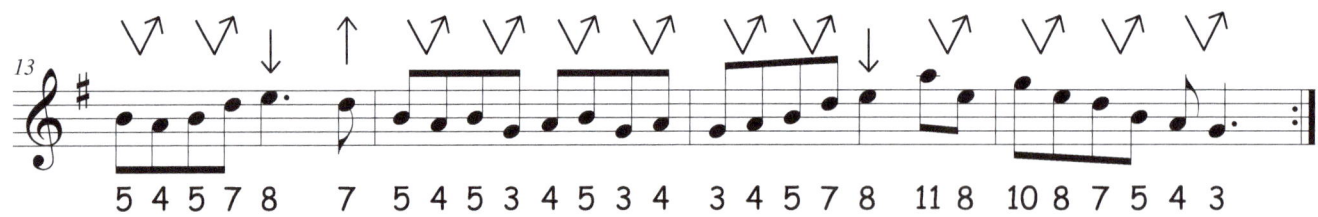

5 4 5 7 8   7   5 4 5 3 4 5 3 4   3 4 5 7 8   11 8 10 8 7 5 4 3

Source: Emmett Lundy, (1864 - 1953) Galax, Virginia

Chord Chart

Part A	G	C	G	D
	G	C	G	D G
Part B	Em	C	Em	D
	Em	C	G	D G

Lost Girl is another tune that "drifted across the big pond." It's most common setting today is from the John Salyer (1882-1952) of Kentucky. Our setting is from a very rare recording of the renown Galax fiddler, Emmett Lundy, who most likely learned it from his mentor Green Leonard (1810-1892).

Emmett Lundy

G Tunes

MAGPIE

Key: G
Tuning: dddd or DGd

Traditional

(sheet music for parts A and B with tablature numbers and bowing marks)

Chord Chart				
Part A	G	G	D	G
	G	G	D	G
Part B	G	G	C	D
	G	G	D	G

There are many versions of this old North Carolina tune. As the old man said, "There ain't just one way to do it." Our version is influenced by the playing of West Virginia fiddler Frank George (1928-2015).

G Tunes

MULVAHILL'S POLKAS #1

Key: G
Tuning: dddd or DGd

Polka 1: Paddy Scanlon's

Traditional Irish

These two rare polkas from County Limerick were recorded in 1978 by the famous fiddler and teacher Martin Mulvihill. Both polkas use gapped scales. The melody of Polka 1 (*Paddy Scanlon's*) has no F# and Polka 2 (*Buddy Furey's*) uses a special gapped scale called the pentatonic scale. It is missing the fourth and seventh tones of the major scale. There are no Cs and no F#s.

MULVAHILL'S POLKAS #2

Polka 2: Buddy Furey's

Traditional Irish

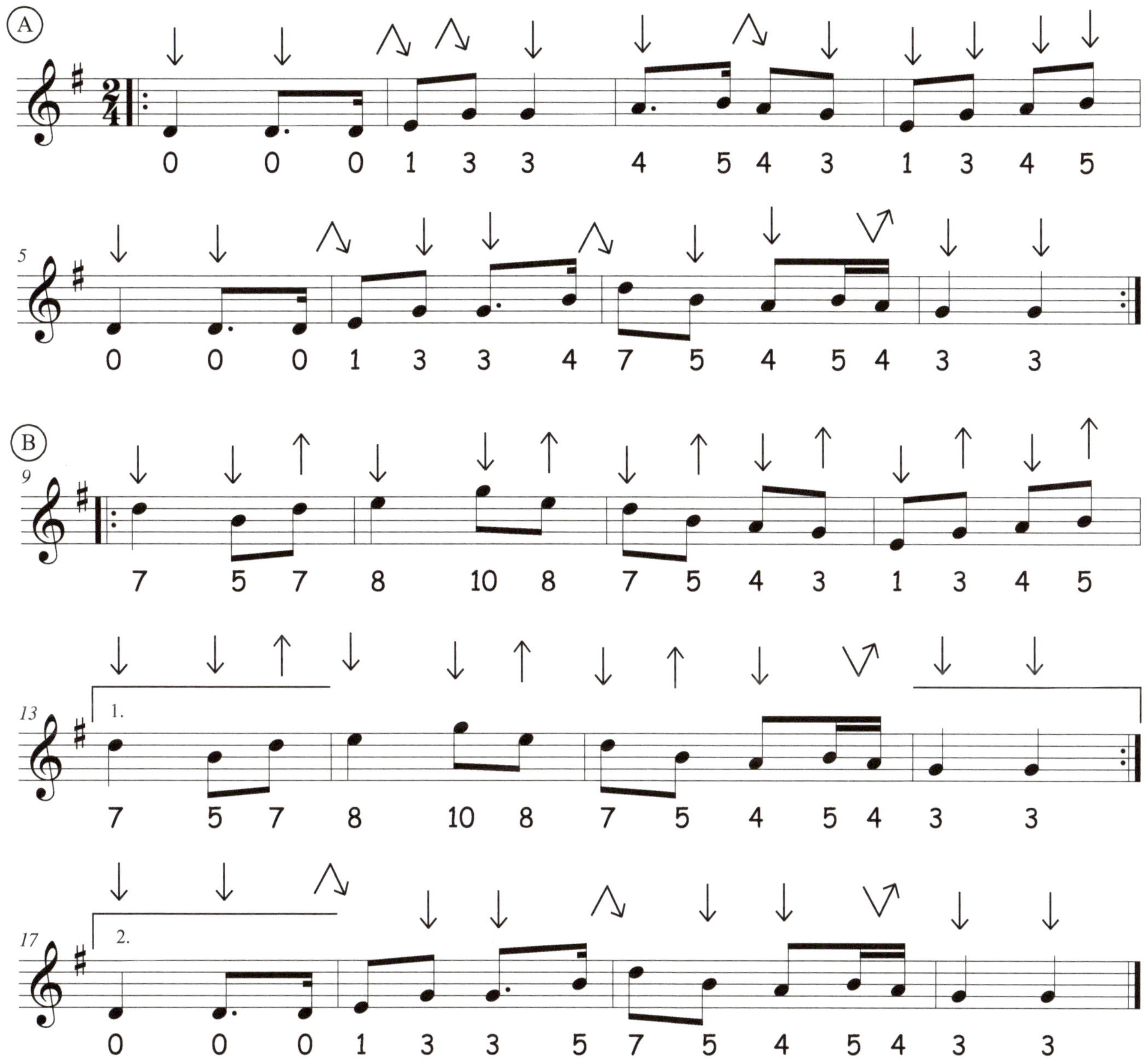

Chord Chart				
Part A	G	G	D	G
	G	G	D	G

B Part	G	C	G	D
1st Ending	G	C	G D	G
2nd Ending	G	C	D	G

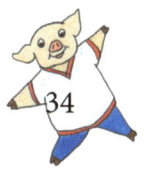

G Tunes

OLD DAD
PIGTOWN FLING / STONEY POINT

Key: G
Tuning: dddd or DGd

Traditional

Source: Luther Davis, (1887-1986)

Chord Chart

Part A	G	G	G	D
	G	G	G	D G
Part B	Em	Em	Em	D
	Em	Em	C	D G

Pigtown Fling! They're playing our tune! Let's Dance!

This tune was first collected and published in 1883 in **Ryan's Mammoth Collection** under its "original" title, *Kelton's Reel*. With Irish collector Francis O'Neill's impetus, the melody leapt across the Atlantic and became an "authentic, ancient Irish tune." The tune has remained melodically consistent over time picking up different names as it spread. The two most common titles are *Stoney Point* and *Pigtown Fling*. In Galax the old 19th and early 20th century fiddlers called it *Old Dad*.

OLD YELLER DOG CAME TROTTIN' THROUGH THE MEETIN' HOUSE

Key: G
Tuning: dddd or DGd

Traditional

Some Lyrics

Old Yeller Dog came trottin' through the Meetin' House, trottin' through the Meetin' House, trottin' through the Meetin' House.
Old Yeller Dog came trottin' through the Meetin' House, Down in Alabam'.

Chord Chart

Part A	G	G	D	G
	G	G	D	G
Part B	G	G	G	Em
	G	G	D	G

My childhood community church near Elkton, Virginia.

(Of course, there are more lyrics but it's also fun to write your own.)

As I was researching the background info about this tune, I came across a reference to the banning of "lap-dogs" in houses of worship in Scotland! Southern churches were also plagued with the problem of dogs fol-lowing their masters to church and taking advantage of front and back doors opened for "cooling" the church on hot Sunday mornings. I actually remember the open doors creating a cool breeze while inviting bees and flies; no dogs in my memory though! We eventually did a fundraiser to purchase screen doors.

PEAR TREE

Key: G
Tuning: dddd or DGd

Traditional

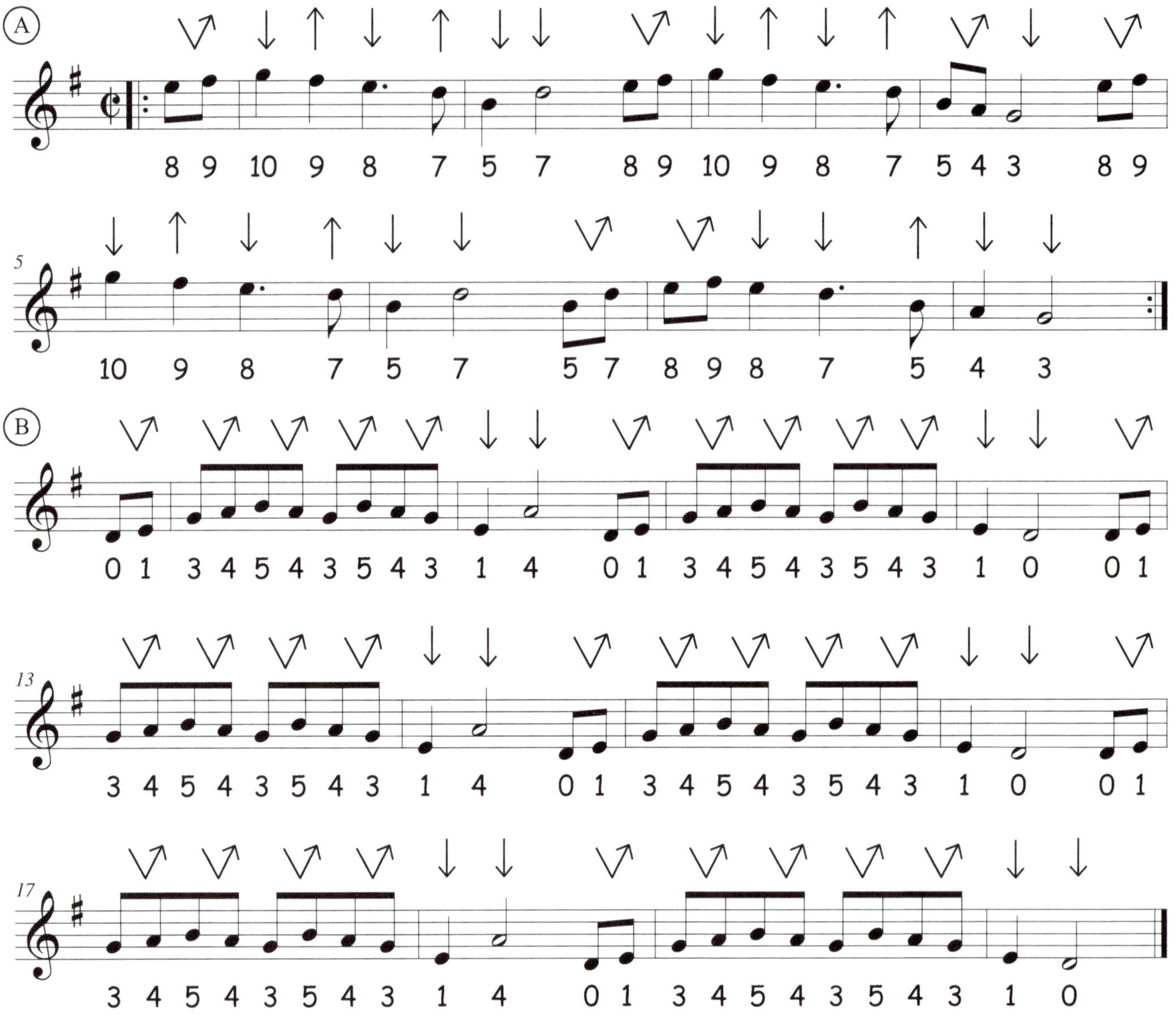

Source: Gaither Wiley Carlton (1901 – 1972), Wilkes County, North Carolina

Chord Chart

Part A	G	D	D	G
	G	D	D	G
B Part (3 Times)	G	Am	D	G

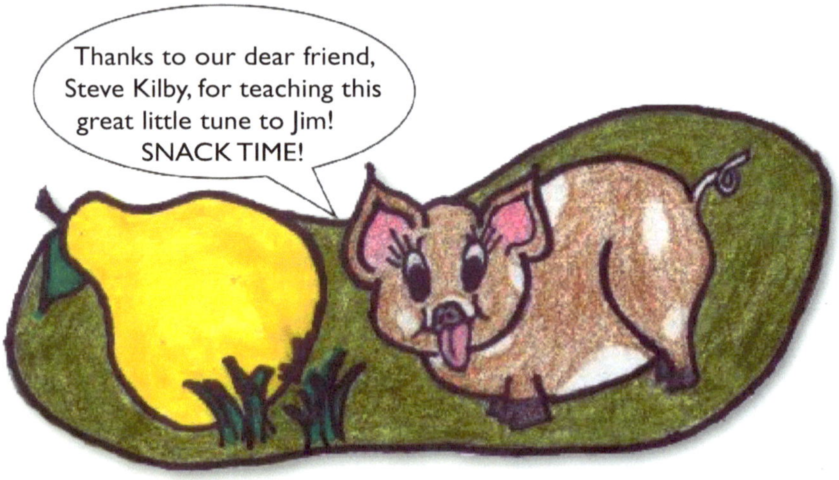

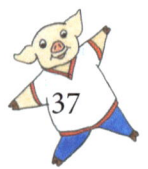

G Tunes

PIG IN A PEN: 1976-77 PUZZLE PIECES

In the summer of 1976, one could hear *Pig in a Pen* being played by many Old Time and Bluegrass bands at every fiddler's convention we attended. It was real easy to pick up by ear with my Bob Mize dulcimer tuned GDd. The first recording of this tune was in 1937 as *Pig at Home in the Pen* by Tennessee's Fiddlin' Arthur Smith, and it quickly became a Bluegrass music standard.

In talking with my mentor, Raymond Melton and other old-timers, I heard that Arthur Smith "claimed" to have written it but it started out as an old-time tune before he recorded it.

In the summer of 1976, Maddie MacNeil also met Raymond and in the **Dulcimer Players News** (Vol.2, No.4, Fall 1976, page 15), there is an article by her entitled *An Interview with Ray (Raymond) Melton*. That was the same summer I first started trying to learn tunes from Raymond. On page 14 there is a small hand drawn illustration by Salem, Virginia dulcimer maker Ken Hamblin telling how to make "An Authentic Appalachian Feather Pick" from a turkey feather. I tried those turkey feathers, but I broke a lot of quills, and I broke a lot of strings. I switched over to using picks made from the bottom of a plastic milk jug. If you cut in the right place, you can get one really good pick. It's a lot of trial and error.

Cut at the places indicated by the arrows.
Strip the barb from the quill.
Use the narrow end to strum.

In 1976, I became determined to stick with the Old Time noter playing. That summer I decided to enter the 1977 dulcimer competition at the Galax Old Fiddlers Convention so Jim and I could get a refund of entrance and camping fees (record money!). The first tune I played in competition was *Pig in a Pen*. Back in our campsite we called it *The Money Back Reel*.

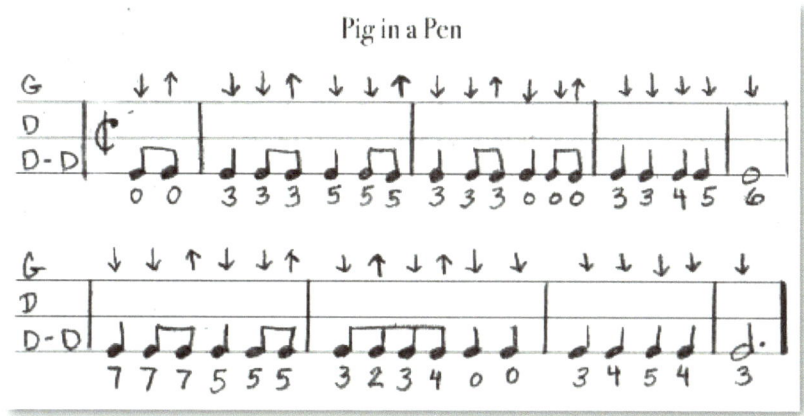

The first dulcimer tablature (TAB) I ever saw was in the **Dulcimer Players News** (DPN). If the TAB for *Pig in a Pen* had appeared in the DPN, it may have looked like this!

Chords:
G / G / G / C
G / G / G / D G

PINEY WOODS GAL

Key: G
Tuning: dddd or DGd

Traditional

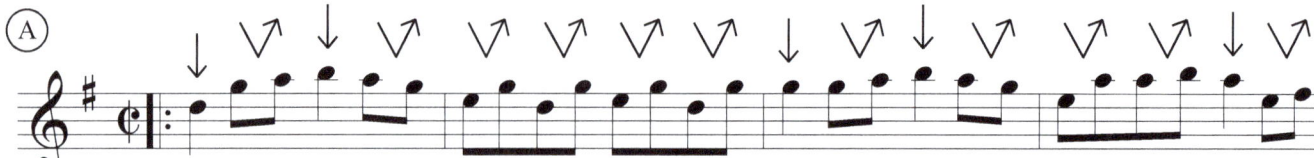
7 10 11 12 11 10 8 10 7 10 8 10 7 10 10 10 11 12 11 10 8 11 11 12 11 8 9

10 10 11 12 11 10 8 10 7 10 8 10 7 8 5 7 5 4 3 1 0 1 3 5 4 3 3   0 1 3 5 4 3 3 4

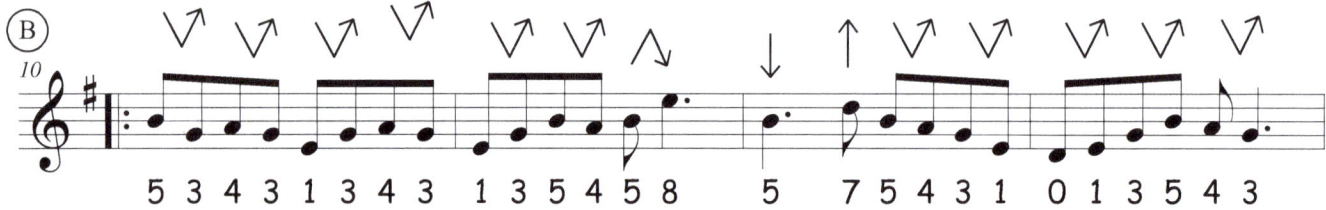
5 3 4 3 1 3 4 3 1 3 5 4 5 8 5 7 5 4 3 1 0 1 3 5 4 3

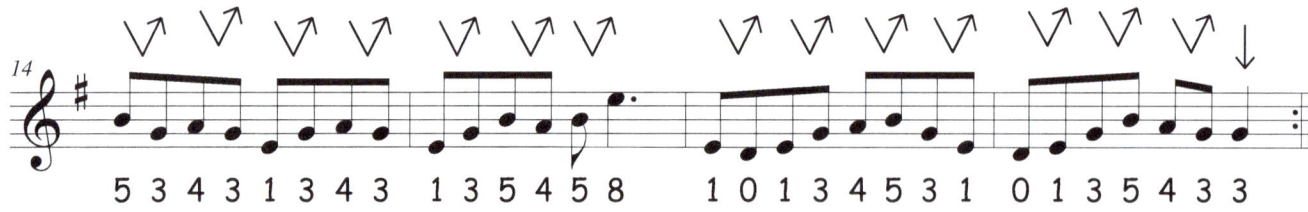
5 3 4 3 1 3 4 3 1 3 5 4 5 8 1 0 1 3 4 5 3 1 0 1 3 5 4 3 3

Source: Luther Davis (1887-1986), Galax, Virginia

Chord Chart

Part A	G	G	G	D
	G	G	D	D G
Part B	Em	Em	Em	D G
	Em	Em	C	D G

Piney Woods Gal is an example of an exceptionally beautiful, quintessential Galax fiddle tune which we learned from the playing of Luther Davis. It has a strong Irish flavor and is believed to be descended from the Irish tune *My Love Is Fair and Handsome* published by Francis O'Neill in the first decade of the 20th century. The tune has an interesting minor key shift like the sun appearing and disappearing on a rainy day. It is one of our most favorite tunes.

In this photo, Luther is standing by the fence separating his land from Emmett Lundy's land.

PRETTIEST LITTLE GIRL IN THE COUNTY

Key: G
Tuning: dddd or DGd

Traditional

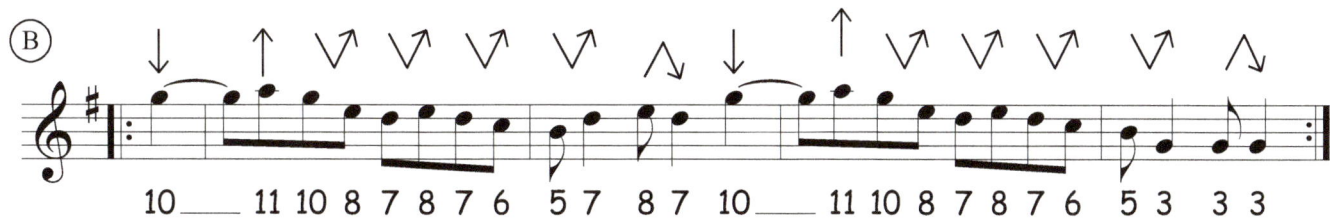

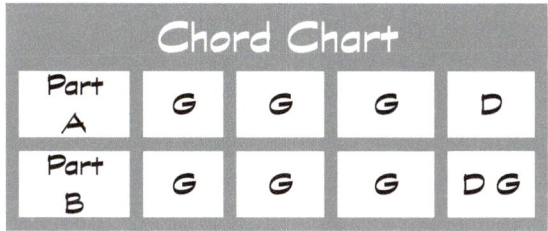

Prettiest Little Girl in the County is so much fun to play! We sometimes call tunes like this "mantra tunes" because once you start playing them, you just want to keep going on and on and on…This 19th century play party tune, also known as *Old Aunt Jenny* and *Prosperity Breakdown*, is fairly common throughout the South. It was documented by Alan and Elizabeth Lomax sometime during the 1930s and 1940s for the Library of Congress.

Some Lyrics

A couple of rhymes from the Skillet Lickers and others are:

Cornstalk fiddle and a pea vine bow,
Gwine to take Sally to the party-o.

Prettiest little girl in the county-o,
Mama and Papa told me so.

All dressed up in calico.
I'm gonna take her to the party-o.

G Tunes

ROSCOE

Key: G
Tuning: dddd or DGd

Traditional

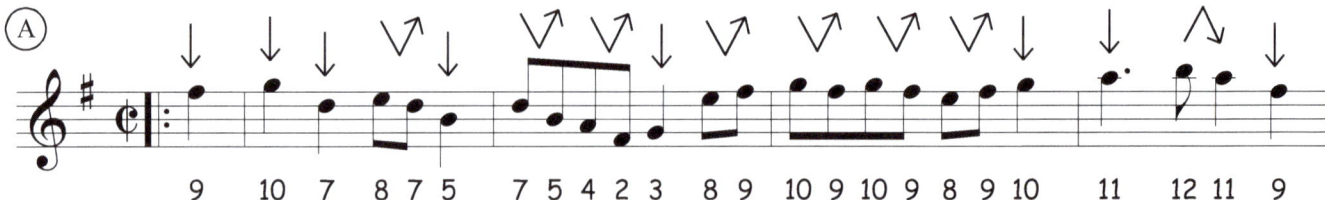

Ⓐ
9 10 7 8 7 5 7 5 4 2 3 8 9 10 9 10 9 8 9 10 11 12 11 9

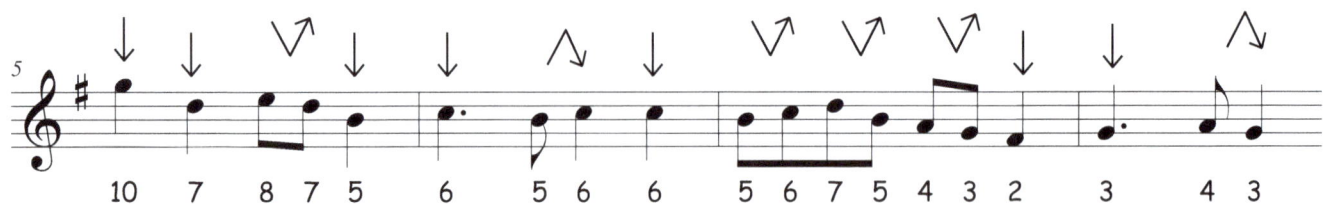

5
10 7 8 7 5 6 5 6 6 5 6 7 5 4 3 2 3 4 3

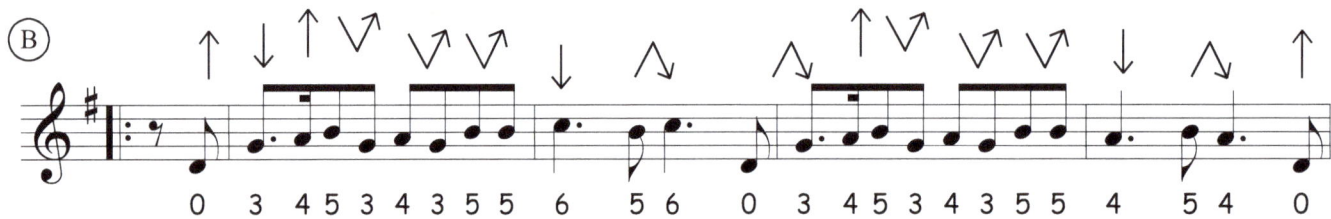

Ⓑ
0 3 4 5 3 4 3 5 5 6 5 6 0 3 4 5 3 4 3 5 5 4 5 4 0

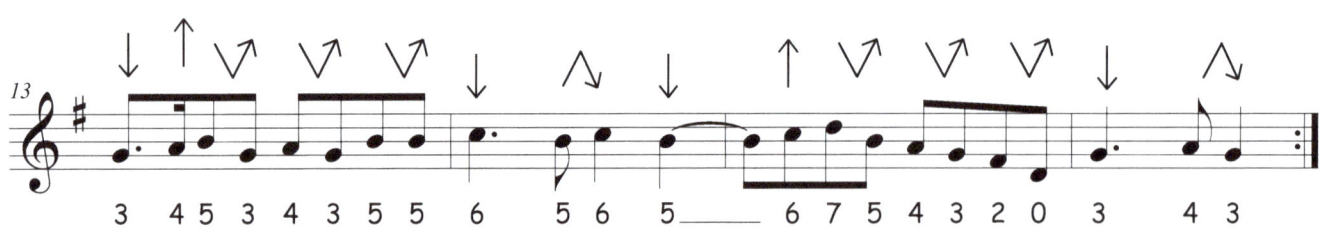

13
3 4 5 3 4 3 5 5 6 5 6 5____ 6 7 5 4 3 2 0 3 4 3

Source: Kyle Creed (1912 -1982), Surry County, North Carolina

Chord Chart

Part A	G	G	G	D
	G	C	G D	G
Part B	G	C	G	D
	G	C	G D	G

Kyle Creed was a legendary banjo maker and player from Surry County, North Carolina. He recorded this tune in Bobby Patterson's Heritage Studio. The folklore that goes with this tune is that as they were doing liner notes, Bobby asked Kyle what was the name of the tune. Kyle replied, "I don't know, but I learned it from Roscoe Russell. Let's call it *Roscoe*."

Roscoe Russell was the father of Bonnie Russell, a child prodigy Galax dulcimer player. Pictured here are Roy Russell (Bonnie's brother), Roscoe Russell, and Bonnie Russell. I feel honored to have played tunes with Kyle and the Russell family.

G Tunes

WALKING THAT PRETTY GIRL HOME

Key: G
Tuning: dddd or DGd

Traditional

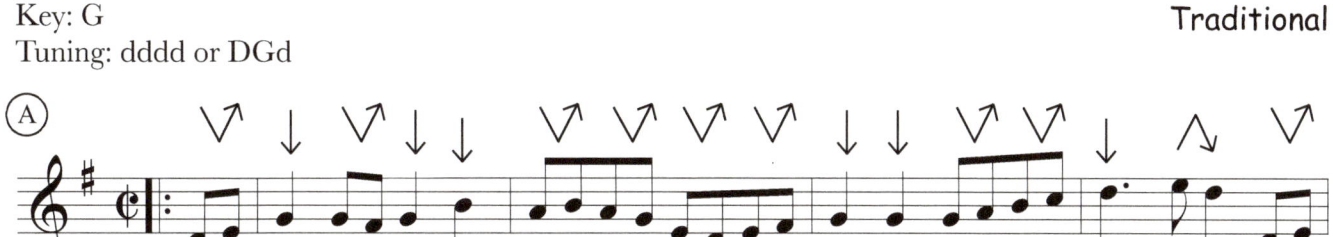
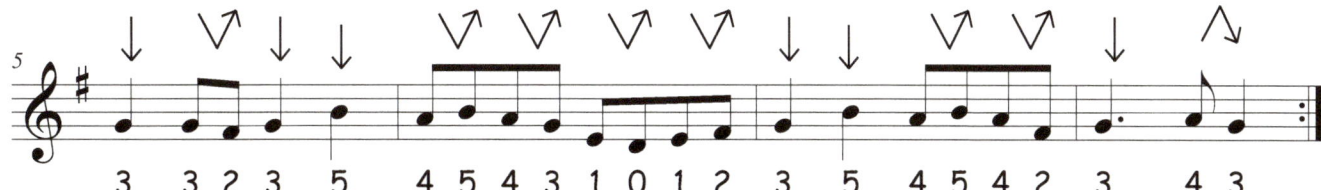
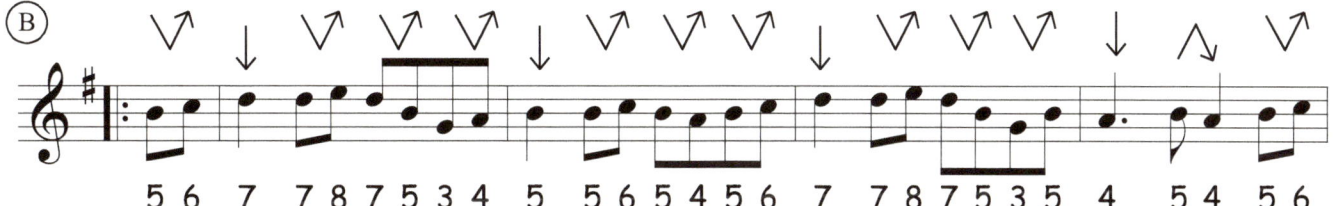
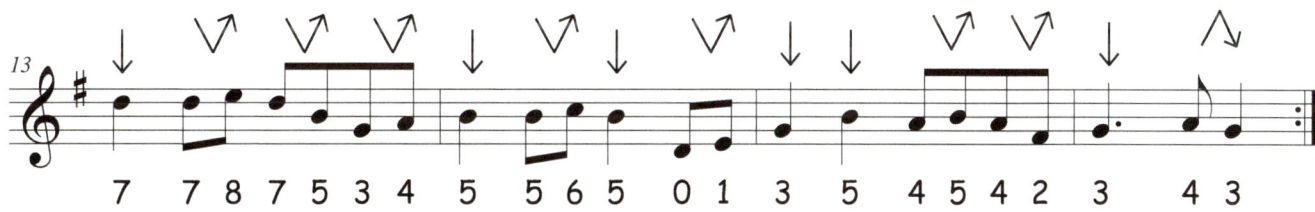

Source: Luther Davis, (1887-1986) Galax, VA

Chord Chart

Part A	G	G	G	D
	G	G	G D	G
Part B	G	G	G	D
	G	G	G D	G

Walking That Pretty Girl Home is another lovely, rare tune from our mentor, Luther Davis. This tune was played by Luther and his contemporaries throughout most of the early half of the 20th century but has almost disappeared since. From the early 1940s until the traditional music boom of the late 1960s and early 1970s, the Galax fiddlers and others throughout the region played it very little if at all. Instruments were stored under beds and in closets for decades due to the drastic changes in popular musical culture. To those of us who are lovers and practitioners of the true Old Time music, it is a blessing that the "old fellers and gals" picked up their instruments again and passed this huge body of traditional tunes and songs on to us.

WAVES ON THE OCEAN
(OLD WOMAN, OLD WOMAN)

Key: G
Tuning: dddd or DGd

Traditional

Chord Chart

Part A	G	C G	C G	D
	G	C G	C	G
Part B	G	G C	D	D G
	G	C	D	D G

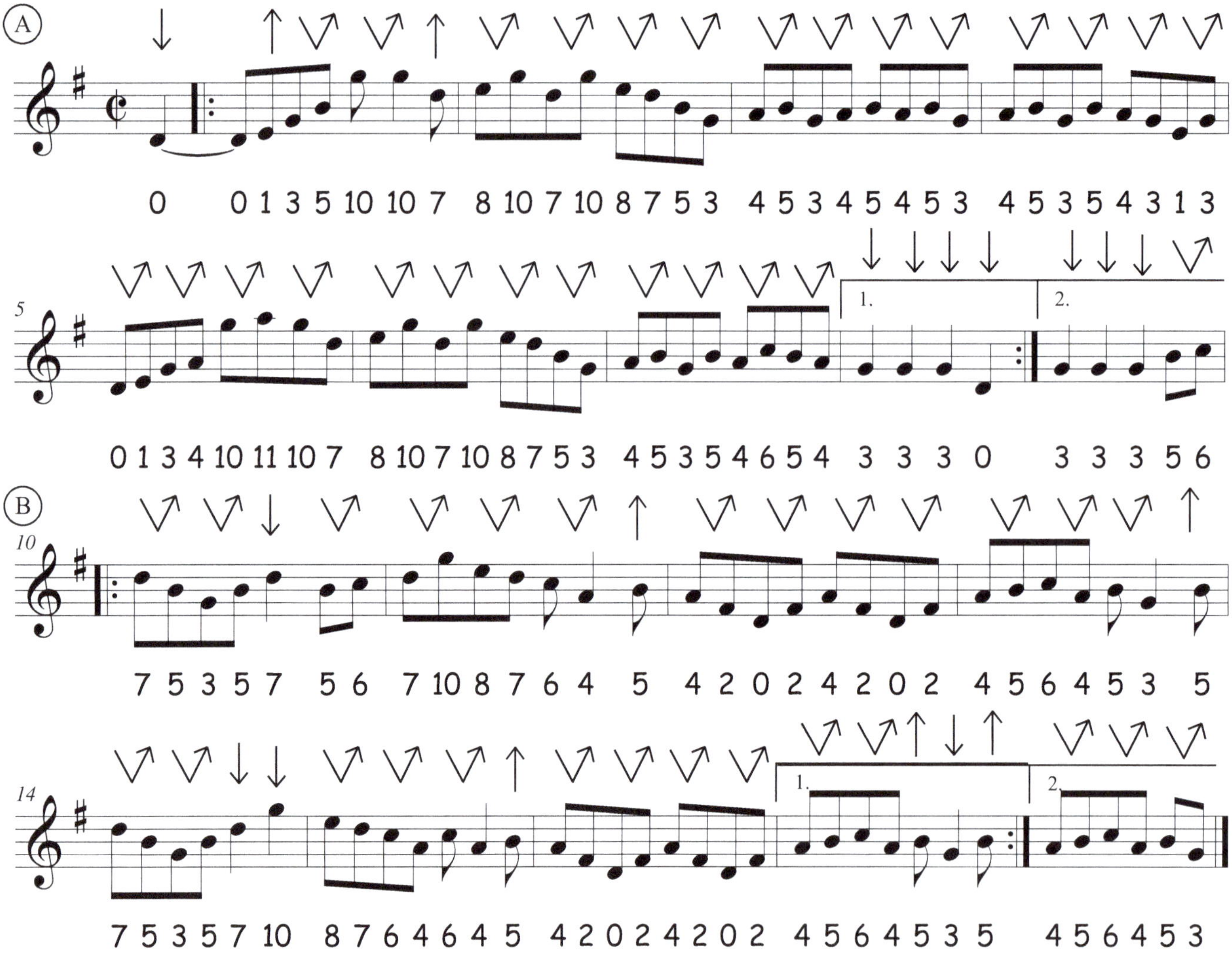

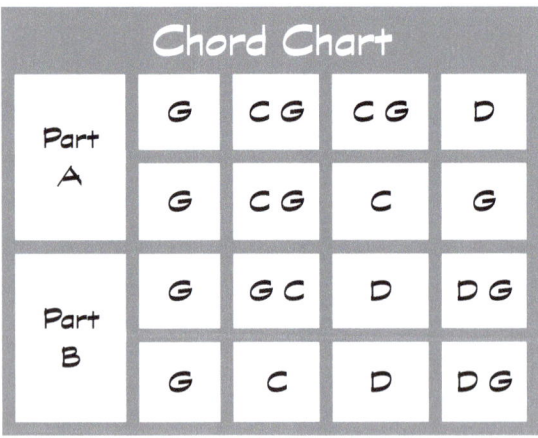

In 1941, Elizabeth Lomax collected this tune for the Library of Congress from the Galax, Virginia, fiddle player Emmett Lundy who lived on the adjoining farm to our fiddle mentor Luther Davis. We played this tune with Luther, and in 1978, 90-year old Luther said, "Old man Emmett Lundy played all those old hornpipe-y tunes and us young fiddlers didn't care for that old stuff." We chuckled. We also chuckled at the lyrics collected from Emmett Lundy.

"Old woman, old woman, don't you want to marry?"
"Speak a little louder, sir, I can barely hear ye."
"Old woman, old woman, don't you want to marry?"
"God Almighty, bless my soul, I just began to hear ye!"

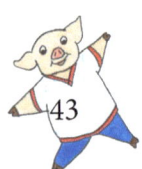

THE DEAF WOMAN'S COURTSHIP
(OLD WOMAN, OLD WOMAN)

Key: G
Tuning: dddd or DGd

Traditional

Chord Chart

Part A	G	G	D	G
	G	G	D	G

Lyrics from Mrs. Emma Early:

Old woman, old woman,
are you fond of smoking?
Speak a little louder, sir,
I'm rather hard of hearing.

Old woman, old woman,
are you fond of carding?
Speak a little louder, sir,
I'm rather hard of hearing.

Old woman, old woman,
don't you want me to court you?
Speak a little louder, sir,
I've just begun to hear you.

Old woman, old woman,
don't you want to marry me?
Lord have mercy on my soul,
I think now I hear you.

The famous English scholar and folksong collector Cecil Sharp did intensive research and collecting of old English folksongs in the Southern Appalachians during the early 20th century. He collected this song on Sept. 9, 1918, in Clinchfield, North Carolina, from Mrs. Emma Early. Lyrics varied in these old songs because they were passed orally through the generations from singer to singer. I have included this particular song because the wonderful fiddle tune, *Waves On the Ocean,* evolved from its melody.

A Tunes

Drive your "Modal A" through the **mudddd** in the old **A**-Modal way!

"This one's in A-modal, boys!" said the fiddler leading the Old Time session. The turning of pegs began on the banjo, and there I sat wondering, "What's A-modal?". Listening to the tunes I realized these were very different from the major tunes I had been playing in G and D.

METHINKS: "Whoa! How can I do that if I'm tuned dddd?"

It was all so VERY confusing. At that time no one knew how to help me. So I figured it out! If I could just change the drones to <u>ee</u> then I should be able to play these tunes. Tuning the drone

A-ish Tunes

strings up to <u>ee</u> worked, but I broke a LOT of strings. In those days capos for dulcimers consisted of a dowel stick held on with a rubber band. They slid off the end of my dulcimer. (Remember page 7?)

Then **ME THINKS**: "If you could change a note by pressing down on the strings, then you should be able to change the note by lifting up the strings." AHA! A little piece of notched wood under the two drones at the first fret could raise the tone up to <u>ee</u>. Happy me! I called it several things in those days: un-capo, half-nut, false nut. I've spread that idea around a lot, and it is now mostly called a false nut.

What does "A-modal" refer to in Old Time music?

These are tunes which are not major or minor. In Appalachian Old Time music, an A tune is most often in Mixolydian mode and the A-modal tunes are most often Dorian mode. I call these A-ish tunes.

Please explain, Ms. Phyllis.

Well, it's easier to play than it is to explain. Just tune to all <u>d</u>s or DGd, put either the capo on the first fret or the false nut under the drone strings, and play all the tunes in this section. That worked for me for years and years, and I had no clue what I was doing. I only knew it worked. But since you asked and there are some inquiring minds who truly want to understand, here goes.

A Tunes

LET'S START WITH TUNING

Tune to all ds or DGdd, then use a false nut or a capo at the first fret.

There are two all D tunings: Bagpipe (Dddd) which has a bass string an octave lower than the other three and Galax (dddd) which has all of the strings at the same gauge and tuned to d beside middle C on the piano.

DGdd tuning is an alternate tuning for the G Tunes in this book. That same tuning can be used for the A-ish Tunes in this section. This is how it works.

FRETBOARD DIAGRAM: Use either a false nut or a capo to change the tone of the two drone strings. Using a false nut allows you to keep the D note for playing. Using the capo eliminates the D note and makes the open tone an E, but still retains the scale.

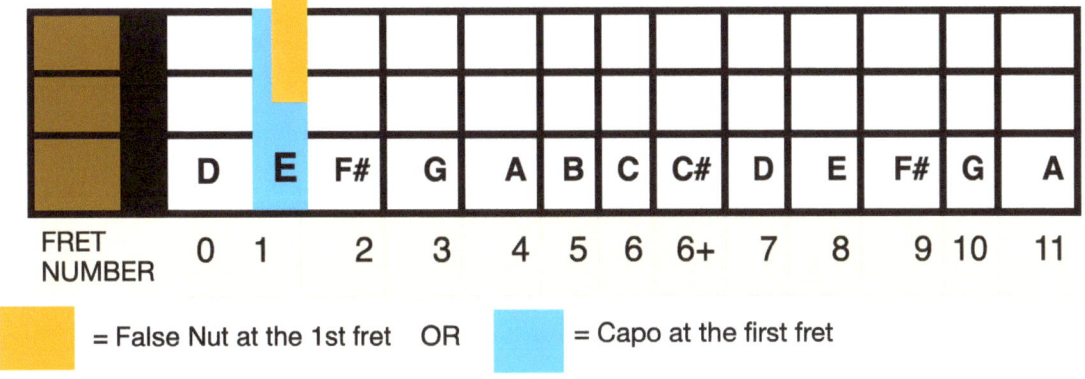

SCALES for the Modes

 **A Ionian**
A B C# D E F# G# A

 A Mixolydian has a flattened seventh tone, no G#; all the Gs are natural.
A B C# D E F# G A

 A Dorian has two flattened notes, no C# and no G#.
A B C D E F# G A

 **A Aeolian** has three flattened notes, no G#, C#, or F#.
A B C D E F G A

Keep that **Modal A** chugging through the mu**dddd**!

Aeolian can be problematic for using the tunings in this book because a one and a half (1.5) fret would be needed. I have been known to scotch tape a straightened paperclip where the 1.5 fret would go and it works fine for a short time. The Aeolian mode is the equivalent of the modern minor scale.

The majority of A-ish tunes in Old Time music are A Mixolydian or A Dorian. That's why a capo or false nut works. You will also come across A Pentatonic tunes with no **d** and no **g** at all.

A Tunes

BETTY LIKENS

Mode: A Dorian
Tuning: dddd, use false nut to make e drones
or DGD capoed @ 1st fret to make EAe

Traditional

Source: Henry Reed (1894-1969), Glen Lyn, Virginia

Chord Chart

Part A	A	A	A	G
Part B	Am	Am	Am	Em
	Am	Am	Am Em	Em A

Oh, Ms. Phyllis! This looks like a G tune in the A-ish section!

It does, doesn't it?

Looking at the Key Signature of *Betty Likens*, one might assume it's in the key of G. Look again. The tune is built on an A scale and resolves on an A, putting it in the Dorian mode. If you look through fiddle tune books, you will see other tunes that have this key signature. The scale and how the tune resolves is most important.

When you are dealing with modal tunes, remember that the job of the key signature is to let you know which notes are sharp, flat, and natural. See "A-ish Scales" for the modes page 51.

Thank you, Sheila, for reminding us of this great tune at Waynesboro White House Session! Good friends, good times, good tunes!

CALLAHAN

A Tunes

Mode: A (Pentatonic Scale)
Tuning: dddd, use false nut to make e drones
or DGd capoed @ 1st fret to make EAe

Traditional

Ⓐ
8 8 9 11 9   11 9 11 9 8 6+   8 9 11 11 13+ 11 8   8

8 9 11 9   11 9 11 9 8 6+   5 4 2 4 1 9   8 6+ 5 6+ 5 4

Ⓑ
4 4 9 8 6+   5 4 5 6+ 5 4 2   1 9 8 6+   5 6+ 5 4

Source: Norman Edmonds (1889-1976), Hillsville, Virginia

Chord Chart

Part A	A	A	A	E A
	A	A	A	A
B Part (3 Times)	A	A	A	E A

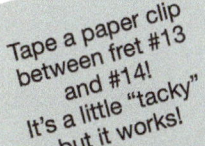

Norman Edmonds (1889-1976) held the fiddle on his chest in the archaic mountain style as he played with his famous band The Old Timers. His vast repertoire included many rare tunes passed down from his grandfather to his father from whom he learned to play. This rich 100-year-old mountain fiddling tradition was recorded by his son, Rush. "Uncle Norm" was truly one of the greats of the Galax/Hillsville fiddling tradition.

48

A Tunes

JUNE APPLE

Mode: A Mixolydian
Tuning: dddd, use false nut to make e drones
or DGd capoed @ 1st fret to make EAe

Traditional

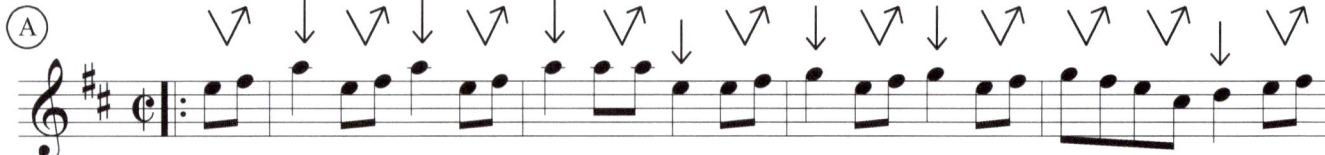

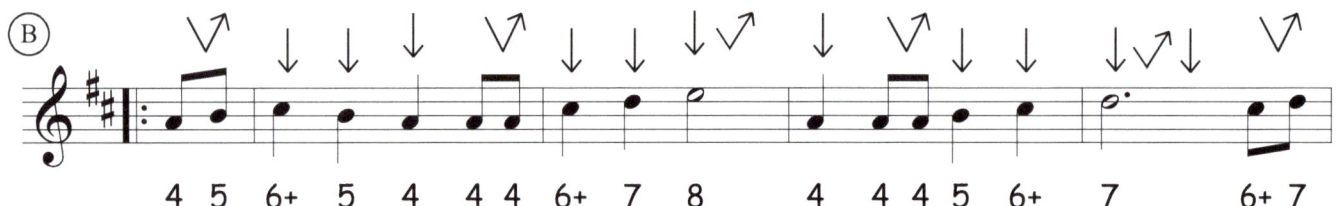

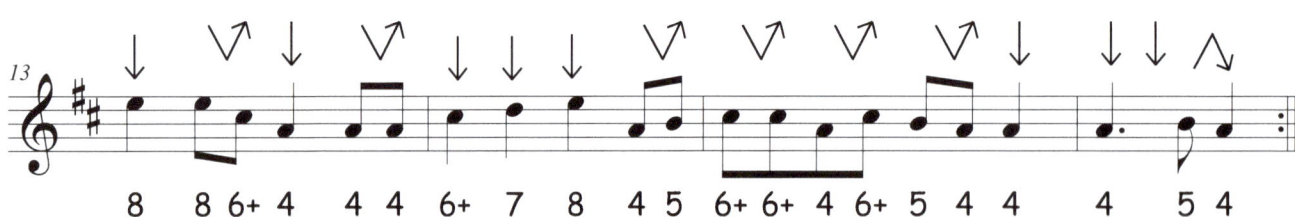

Chord Chart

Part A	A	A	G	G
	A	A	A E	A

Part B	A	A	A	D
	A	A	A E	A

Lyrics (sung to the B part of the tune)

Well, I wish I was a June Apple,
Hangin' on a tree,
Every time my sweetheart passed,
She'd take a little bite of me.

Charlie, he's a nice young man,
Charlie, he's a dandy!
Charlie, he's a nice young man,
Feeds the girls on candy.

Over the river to feed my sheep,
Over the river, Charlie,
Over the river to feed my sheep,
Feed them on Barley.

Also known as the Carolina Red June, the June Apple blooms late for an early apple and is the sweetest in early July. The flesh of the apple is white with red stains. The June Apple was often used for pie and cider. If the season was perfect, the tree would bloom again and form fruit in the fall as well.

LITTLE DUTCH GIRL

A Tunes

Key: A major (Ionian)
Tuning: dddd, use false nut to make e drones
or DGd capoed @ 1st fret to make EAe

Traditional

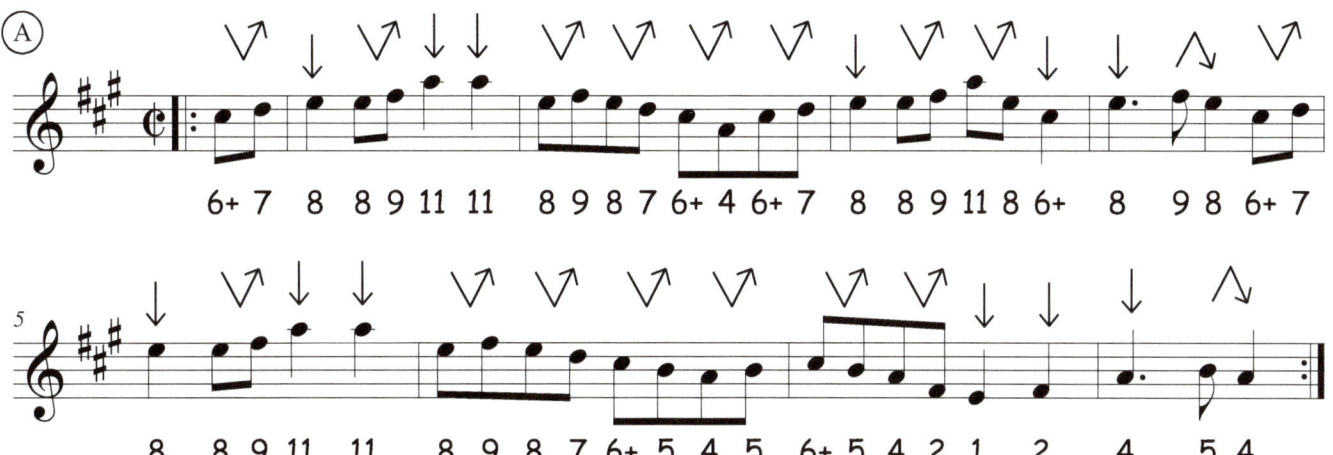

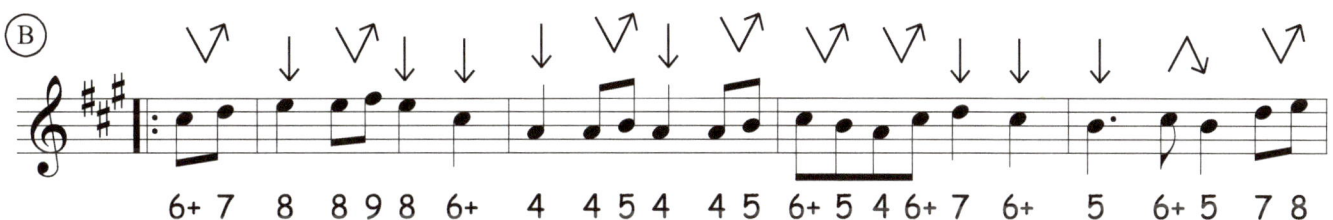

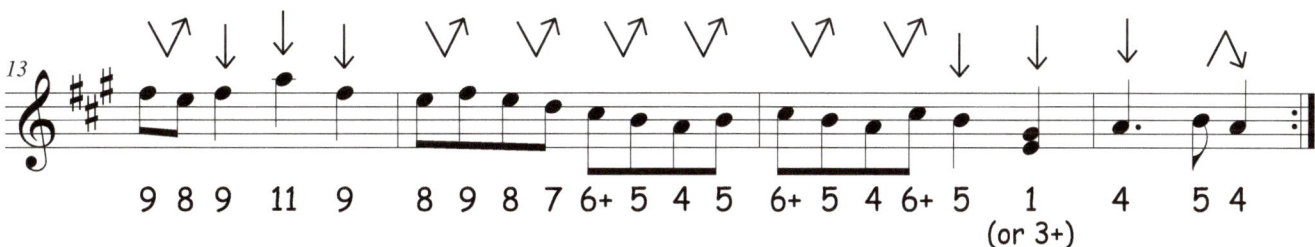

Chord Chart				
Part A	A	A	A	E
	A	A	A E	A
Part B	A	A	A	E
	D	A	A E	A

Caution: This is an Ionian tune, however, I have no G# (fret 3.5) on my dulcimer so I play an E where the G# falls which fits fine within the E chord.

A Tunes

LITTLE RABBIT

Key: A major (Gap Scale: no Gs)
Tuning: dddd, use false nut to make e drones
or DGd capoed @ 1st fret to make EAe

Traditional

A) 8 9 11 11 8 9 8 4 8 11 11 8 12 8 9 11 11 8 9 11 11 9 8 6+ 6+ 6+

B) 8 9 8 6+ 4 5 4 8 9 8 6+ 5 4 6+ 8 9 8 6+ 4 5 4 8 9 8 6+ 5 4

C) 1 2 4 5 4 6+ 8 6+ 4 5 4 6+ 1 2 4 5 4 6+ 8 9 11 8 6+ 5 4

D) 6+ 7 8 8 9 9 8 6+ 6+ 7 8 9 11 9 8 6+ 6+ 7

   8 8 9 9 8 6+ 6+ 5 4 2 1 1 2 4

E) 6+ 5 4 2 1 1 8 6+ 6+ 5 4 2 1 1 2 4

A Tunes

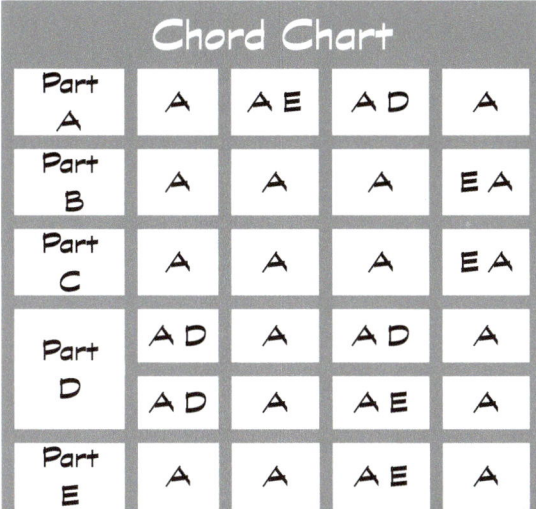

Chord Chart

Part A	A	A E	A D	A
Part B	A	A	A	E A
Part C	A	A	A	E A
Part D	A D	A	A D	A
	A D	A	A E	A
Part E	A	A	A E	A

Most versions of this tune are based on an early 1920s recording by Crockett's Kentucky Mountaineers. The tune has elements of several tunes from the Blue Ridge Mountains where it probably originated and then traveled west with settlers.

Lyrics are sung to Part D.

*Little Rabbit, where's your Mammy?
Little Rabbit, where's your Mammy?
I want to see your Mammy,
Tell me, Rabbit, where's your Mammy?*

Jim and I most likely added this to our "To Be Learned" list a long time ago when we heard it played by Roger Sprung's group at Galax. It kept being moved to the bottom of the list probably because it is a five-part tune AND the parts sounded like other tunes which sometimes confused us. During the Covid19 lock down in our retirement village, we learned a lot of "new to us" tunes and happily shared them with our band mates on Zoom sessions.

Our "pick up" band at a fiddlers' convention, 1981

Highlander String Band, 2019
(Brent Holl, Phyllis, Jim, & Gene Bowlen)

OH, MISS LIZA, POOR GAL

Key: A major (Pentatonic scale)
Tuning: dddd, use false nut to make e drones
or DGd capoed @ 1st fret to make EAe

Traditional

A Part tab numbers:
11 9 8 9 6+ 6+ 5 5 4 11 9 8 6+ 9
11 9 8 9 6+ 6+ 5 5 4 6+ 5 1 2 4

B Part tab numbers:
6+ 6+ 6+ 6+ 5 4 6+ 6+ 5 4 2
5 5 5 5 6+ 5 5 5 6+ 5 1 2 4

Chord Chart

Part A	A	A	A	D
	A	A	AE	A
Part B	A	A	A	D
	E	E	E	A

Verses (sung on B Part)

1. Went up on the mountain,
To give my horn a blow.
Thought I heard Miss Liza sayin'
"Yonder comes my beau!"

2. Yonder comes my true love.
How do I know?
Tell him (her) by them sparklin' eyes,
Shining bright like gold!

Chorus (sung to A Part)

Oh, Miss Liza,
pretty little gal,
Oh, Miss Liza Jane.
Oh, Miss Liza,
pretty little gal,
Ridin' on that train.

OLD MOTHER FLANNAGAN

A Tunes

Mode: A Ionian (Major)
Tuning: dddd, use false nut to make e drones
or DGd capoed @ 1st fret to make EAe

Traditional

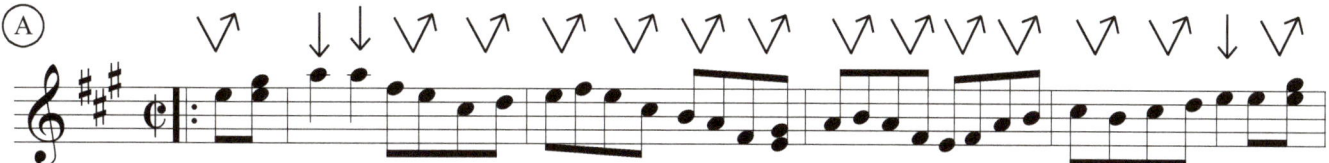

Ⓐ
8 8* 11 11 9 8 6+ 7 8 9 8 6+ 5 4 2 1* 4 5 4 2 1 2 4 5 6+ 5 6+ 7 8 8 8*

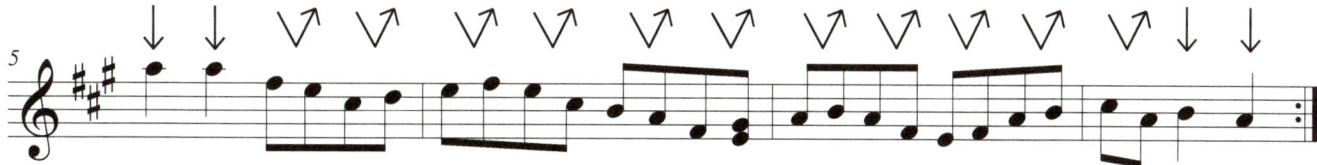

11 11 9 8 6+ 7 8 9 8 6+ 5 4 2 1* 4 5 4 2 1 2 4 5 6+ 4 5 4

Ⓑ
1 2 4 5 4 2 1 2 4 5 6+ 6+ 4 5 4 2 1* 4 5 4 2 1 2 4 5 6+ 4 5 4

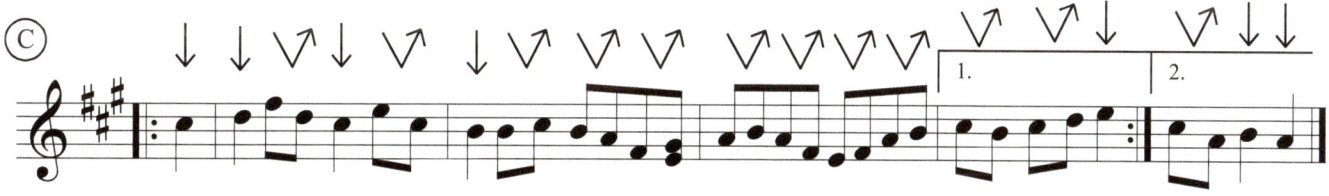

Ⓒ
6+ 7 9 7 6+ 8 6+ 5 5 6+ 5 4 2 1* 4 5 4 2 1 2 4 5 6+ 5 6+ 7 8   6+ 4 5 4

**If you have a 3.5 and 10.5 fret you can play the G# notes.
If not, substitute the E notes as indicated by the 1* an 8*.**

Chord Chart

Part A	A	A	A	E	
	A	A	A	E A	
Part B	A	A	A	E A	
Part C	D A	E	A	1. E	2. E A

Old Mother Flannagan is a popular tune in our local Old Time and Irish sessions. If Jim and I start it, we use this three-part version we believe came from the fiddling of Jack Tuttle. Most fiddlers have "squared" this tune up by combining Parts B and C into a single eight-bar part repeated. This seems to work better for contra dances.

54

A Tunes

OLE TIME JOHN HENRY

Mode: A Mixolydian
Tuning: dddd, use false nut to make e drones
or DGd capoed @ 1st fret to make EAe

Traditional

(A) 8 9 10 9 8 6+ 11 12 11 8 9 10 9 8 7 6+ 4 4 5 4 8 9

10 9 8 7 6+ 11 11 10 9 8 7 8 8 9

10 9 8 7 6+ 11 12 11 8 9 10 9 8 7 6+ 4

(B) 8 9 10 9 8 7 6+ 6 5 4 2 4 5 6+ 6 6+ 4 2 8 9

(slide from 5 to 6+, and from 6 to 6+)

10 9 8 7 6+ 4 2 1 2 4 5 4

55

A Tunes

Chord Chart

Part A	A	A	A	A
	A	A	E	E
	A	A	A	A
Part B	A	A	A	F#m
	A	A	A	A

Richard Bowman and his band, The Slate Mountain Ramblers, at the 2021 Galax Fiddlers' Convention.

Jim and I learned this version of *Ole Time John Henry* from our long time fiddling friend, Richard Bowman, and his band The Slate Mountain Ramblers. Richard has a treasure trove of great tunes from legendary fiddlers in the area where he was raised, folks like Tommy Jarrell, Fred Cockeram, Taylor Kimble, etc. Thanks for the memories, Richard. Here's to more fiddle tune sessions for all of us!

The Merriam-Webster dictionary defines Tall Tale as "a story that is very difficult to believe; a greatly exaggerated story."

My fascination with American tall-tale heroes of the 1800s began with a postal delivery from Weekly Reader Children's Book Club, *Tall Tales of America* (1958), written by Irwin Shapiro and illustrated by Al Schmidt. I read this book over and over. Later, as a teacher, I shared it with my second grade classes. It sang the praises of America's workers of all ethnicities which celebrated the idea of America as a great melting pot.

John Henry ballads began circulating in the 1870's and many historians believe the stories refer to a real railroad worker who used a "nine pound hammer" to drive steel in a race against the "new" steam-powered rock drilling machine invented to speed up the laying of railway tracks. There is a plaque honoring the memory of John Henry at West Bend Tunnel in West Virginia, as well as in Virginia and Alabama, claiming him as their own.

The songs and stories of the tall-tale heroes have been used to honor the best of the worker's gritty spirit in the face of continuing modern industrialization.

A Tunes

RED HAIRED BOY

Mode: A Mixolydian
Tuning: dddds and use false nut on drones
or DGD capoed @ first fret to make EAE

Traditional

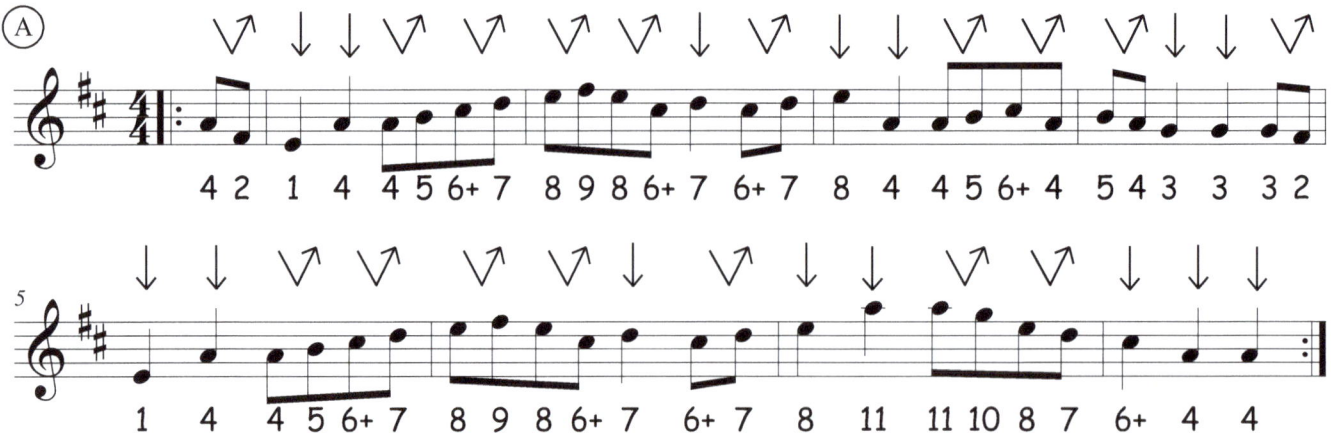

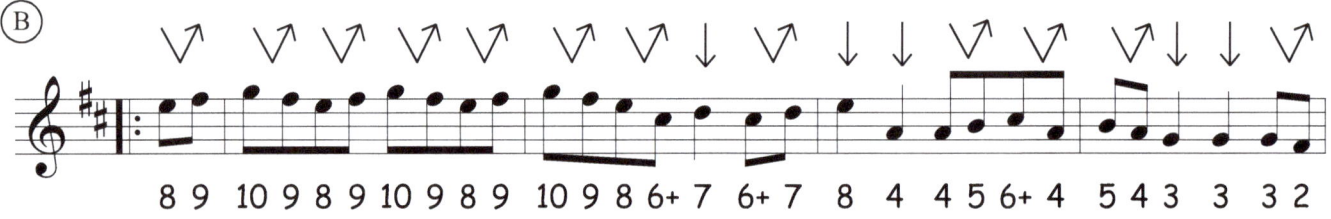

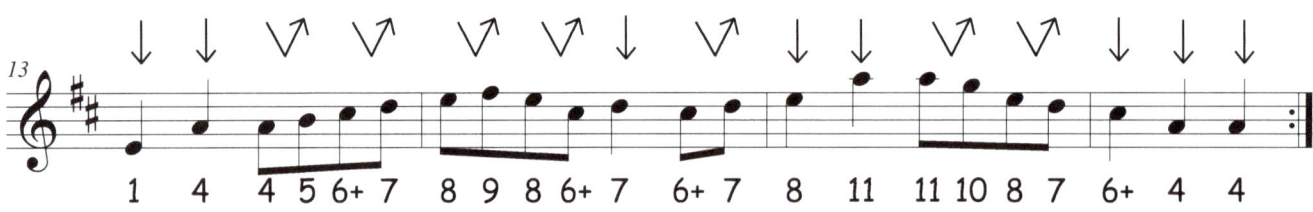

Chord Chart				
Part A	A	A D	A	G
	A	A D	A	E A
Part B	G	G	A	G
	A	A D	A	E A

Irish, Scottish, English, American, Canadian…
Oh, yeah! This tune is welcome everywhere!

Fine memories of Sunday afternoons at Francesco's Irish Session

A Tunes

SANTA ANNA'S RETREAT

Mode: A Mixolydian/Dorian
Tuning: dddd, use false nut to make e drones
or DGD capoed @ 1st fret to make EAe

Traditional

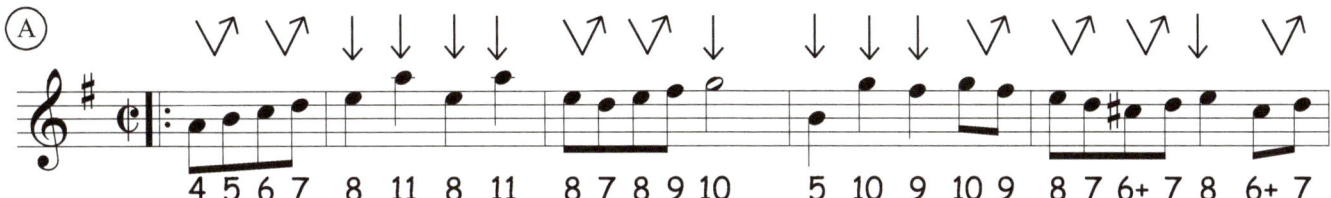

4 5 6 7   8 11 8 11   8 7 8 9 10   5 10 9 10 9   8 7 6+ 7 8 6+ 7

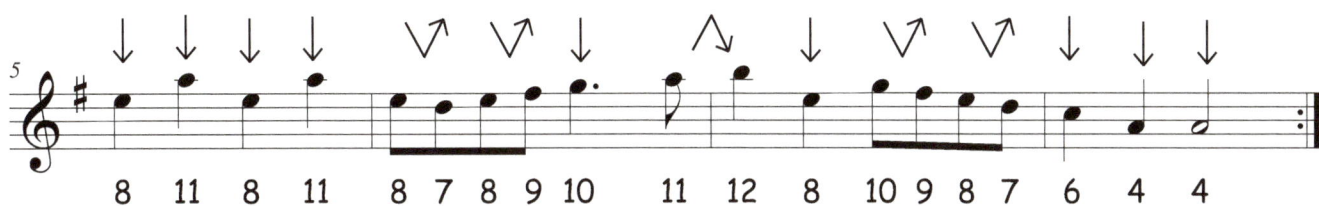

8 11 8 11   8 7 8 9 10   11 12 8   10 9 8 7   6 4 4

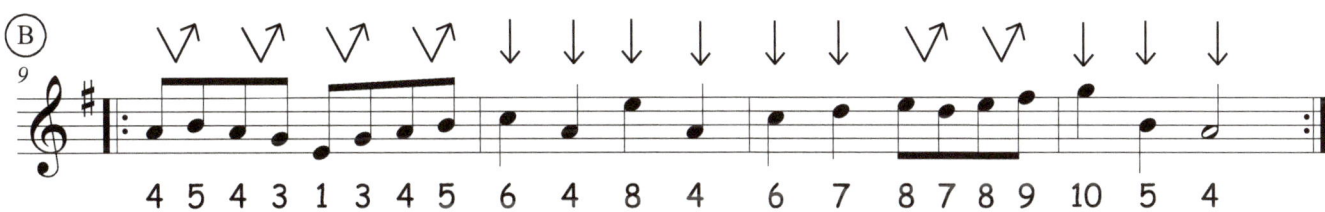

4 5 4 3 1 3 4 5   6 4 8 4   6 7   8 7 8 9 10 5 4

Source: Henry Reed (1884-1968), Glen Lyn, Virginia

Chord Chart

Part A	A	A G	G	A
	A	A G	G	Am
Part B	Am	Am	Am	G Am

This is another tune from the seminal Virginia fiddler, Henry Reed, and refers to the president of Mexico and commander of its army, Antonio Lopez de Santa Anna (1794-1876). Reed learned the tune from his men-tor, neighboring fife player and fiddler Quince Dillion (b. 1813), who served as a fifer in the Mexican American War with the 166th Virginia Militia during the Civil War. When Reed was just a boy, he would sneak off from home to visit "Old Man" Quince Dillion to learn new tunes.

This is a fine crooked tune that I didn't even realize was crooked until I wrote it out! Some fiddlers have "squared it up" so it is usable for square dancing.

A Tunes

SOURWOOD MOUNTAIN

Mode: A Mixolydian
Tuning: dddd, use false nut to make e drones
or DGd capoed @ 1st fret to make EAe

Traditional
(Fiddle Version)

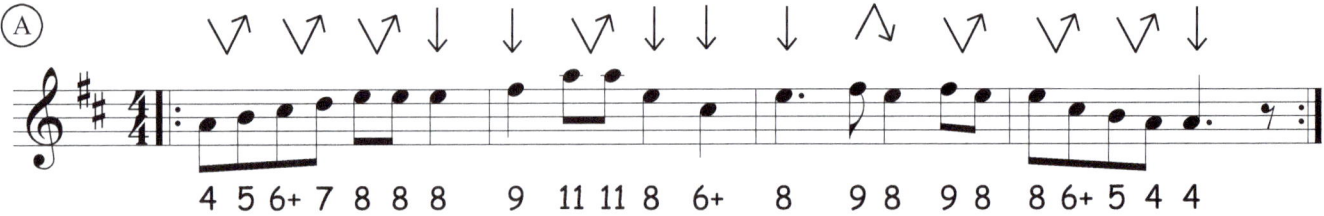

4 5 6+ 7 8 8 8   9 11 11 8 6+   8   9 8 9 8   8 6+ 5 4 4

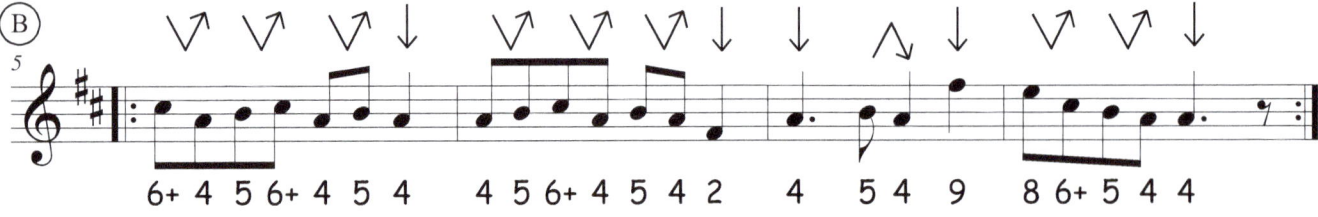

6+ 4 5 6+ 4 5 4   4 5 6+ 4 5 4 2   4   5 4   9   8 6+ 5 4 4

Chord Chart				
A Part	A	A	A	E7 A
B Part	A	A	A	E7 A

A passel of lyrics for this tune/song have been floating around in Appalachian hollars!

Here are the ones I sing:

Chickens crowin' on Sourwood Mountain,
Hey, de ding dang, did-dle-i-day
So many pretty girls I can't count them,
Hey, de ding dang, did-dle-i-day!

My true love's a blue-eyed daisy, hey...
She won't work and I'm too lazy, hey...

My true love lives in the hollar, hey...
She won't come and I won't foller, hey...

My true love lives over the river, hey...
A few more jumps and I'll be with her, hey...

*Why don't you get yourself a **real** instrument?*

59

A Tunes

SULLIVAN'S POLKA

Mode: A Mixolydian
Tuning: dddd, use false nut to make e drones
or DGd capoed @ 1st fret to make EAe

Terry Teahan - Irish

[Musical notation for Part A, measures 1-4]
11 11 9 8 6+ 11 9 8 6+ 11 9 8 6+ 5 4

[Musical notation for Part A, measures 5-8, with 1st and 2nd endings]
11 11 9 8 6+ 11 6+ 8 5 6+ 5 4 4   5 4 4 5

[Musical notation for Part B, measures 10-13]
6+ 8 8 6+ 7 9 9 8 6+ 8 8 4 6+ 5 5

[Musical notation for Part B, measures 14-17, with 1st and 2nd endings]
6+ 8 8 6+ 7 9 9 8 6+ 8 5 6+ 5 4 4 5   5 4 4

Chord Chart

Part A	A	A	A	E
	A	A	A E	E A

Part B	A	D	A	E
	A	D	A E	A

Bill Sullivan's Polka is a favorite local Irish session tune. It was composed by the late Terry "Cuz" Teahan (1905-1989) prior to leaving Ireland in 1928. He was a student of the late Padraig O'Keefe. In Ireland it took on the name of a local Kerry fiddler named Bill Sullivan. In this country Teahan always referred to it as *Mickey Chewing Bubble Gum*.

A Tunes

TATER PATCH

Mode: A Mixolydian
Tuning: dddd, use false nut to make e drones
or DGd capoed @ 1st fret to make EAe

Traditional/Charlie Lowe

Play the B part 3 times.

Source: Tommy Jarrell (1901-1985), Surry County, North Carolina

Chord Chart

Part A	G	G	A	A
	G	G	A E	A
Part B	E	E	A	A

Tater Patch is an interesting tune from the reper-toire of the great Old Time fiddler, Tommy Jarrel. It was composed between 1910 and 1920 by either a banjo player Ike Leonard or fiddler Charlie Lowe. The stories vary considerably. The one consistency is that the composer was working in his potato patch when the melody came to him. He immediately threw down his hoe and ran to the house to grab his instrument and play it before he forgot it.

If one draws enough pictures of pigs, then pretty soon one will see pigs everywhere.

I found potatoes at the local produce stand that looked like pigs so I bought 'em!

UNDAUNTED NOTER

Mode: A Dorian and Mixolydian
Tuning: dddd, use false nut to make e drones
or DGD capoed @ 1st fret to make EAe

Phyllis Gaskins

Chord Chart

Part A	Am	G	Am	Em Am
	Am	G	Am G	Em Am
Part B	A	A	D A	E
	A	A	D A	E A

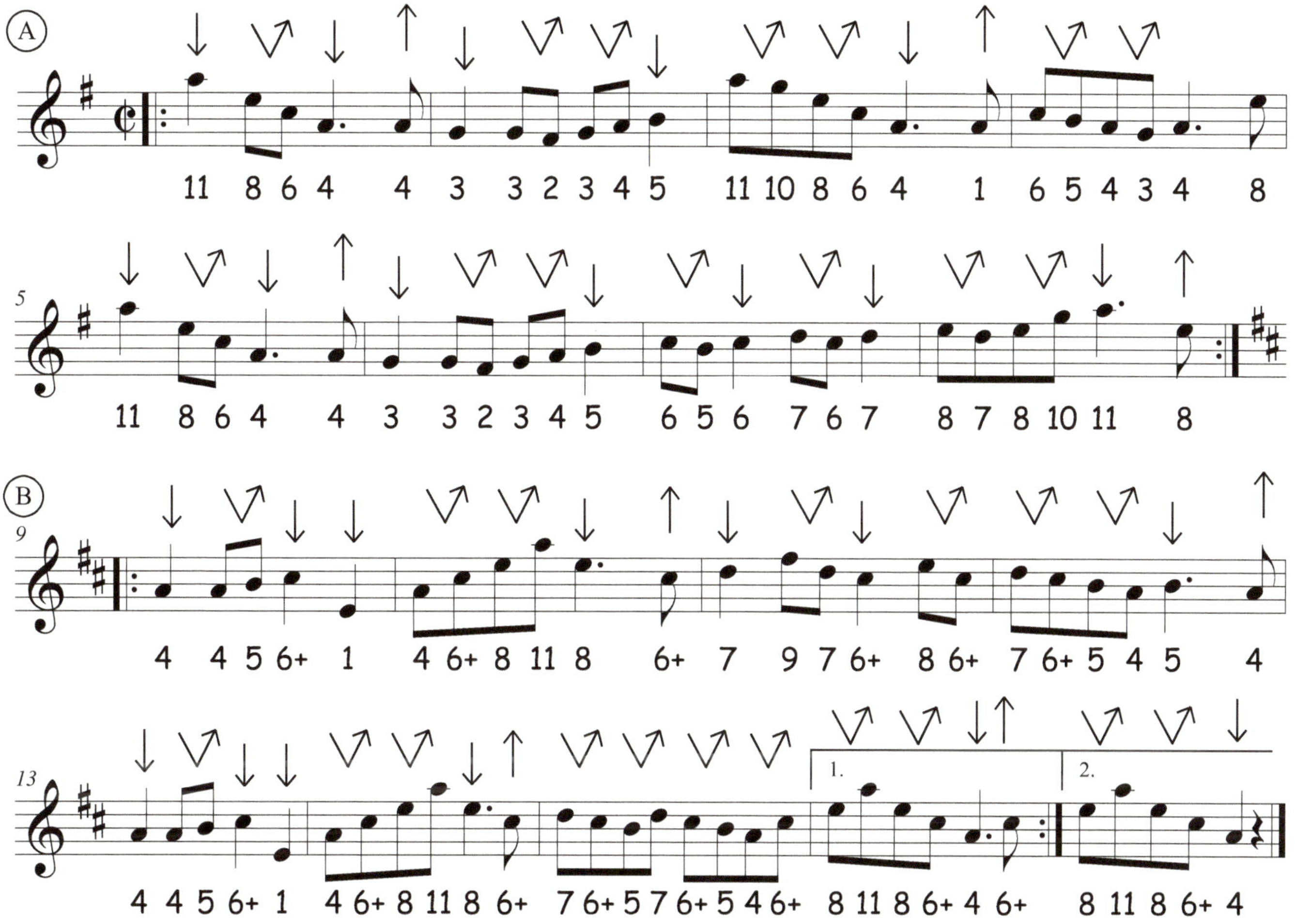

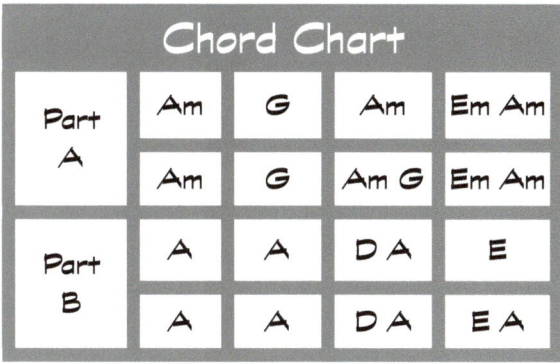

!?!?!? Undaunted Noter? Why? How? I miscalculated! Oh! No! I had allotted one page for *Walsh's Hornpipe*, and it's gonna take two!! Aha! I'll write a tune to go in between *Tater Patch* and *Walsh's Hornpipe*.

I needed a title beginning with U. *Undaunted* I AM! Yes, I am. *Noter:* a person who takes notes (Yes); a person who notes the mountain dulcimer with a stick (Yes)!

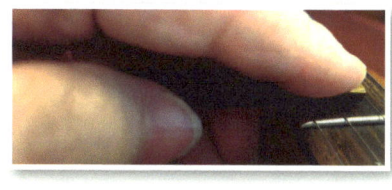

This new tune had to use an A-ish Mode. A fiddle tune usually has two parts. Since an undaunted person usually has a problem, the mood of the A Part expresses that (Dorian). The mood of the B Part then needs to feel successful (Mixolydian).

Fiddle tunes often have a pattern. Measures 1 and 2 form phrase one (question) with measures 3 and 4 responding to phrase one (answer). Then measures 1 and 2 are often repeated in measures 5 and 6 to create phrase three (same question). Measures 7 and 8 have a different pattern (different answer) to end the A Part. The same is generally true for the B Part.

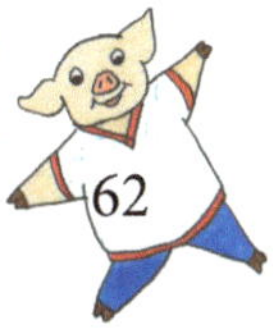

A Tunes

WALSH'S HORNPIPE

Key: A major (Gap Scale: no Gs)
Tuning: dddd, use false nut to make e drones
or DGd capoed @ 1st fret to make EAe

Traditional

A Tunes

Chord Chart

Part A	A	Bm	A	E
	A	Bm	A	E A
Part B	A	A	Bm	E
	A	Bm	A	E A

Walsh's Hornpipe is a delightful tune more commonly played in Ireland than here in the states. Interestingly enough, there are a couple of other tunes with the same title from the US and Scotland.

This wonderful Irish hornpipe comes from the playing of the great, legendary County Kerry fiddler Dennis Murphy (1910-1974). Murphy may have gotten it from fiddle master Padraig O'Keefe (1887-1963). County Kerry is mostly known for its polkas and slides, but it can also boast of wonderful hornpipes and reels. *Walsh's Hornpipe* is one of the best!

Many musical memories! Thanks *dear* friends.

64

Two-Key Tunes

TWO-KEY TUNES!

That tune is in two keys! What should I do?

Raymond Melton: Why, that's no problem at all on my delcimore!

With the traditional Galax tuning of dddd
or the bagpipe tuning of Ddd(d) on a regular three (or four) string dulcimer,
it is quite easy to play a tune with one part in the key of G
and the other part in the key of D.

It's simple!
You see, the key of D starts on the open string and uses the 6+ fret for C#.

Note:	D	E	F#	G	A	B	C#	D
Fret #	0	1	2	3	4	5	6+	7

The three tunes in this section start in the key of G and then switch to the key of D in the B Part.

Yeah, the key of G starts on the third fret and uses fret 6 for C natural. Easy peasy and no **mudddd** to worry about!

Note:	G	A	B	C	D	E	F#	G
Fret #	3	4	5	6	7	8	9	10

NOTE: You may want to go back and play the A Part one time through to end the tune.

Two-Key Tunes

BELFAST POLKA

Key: G and D
Tuning: dddd or Ddd(d)

Traditional

(A) [sheet music line 1]
0 0 0 0 1 0   5 5 5 5 6 5   4 4 4 4 5 4   3 1 0

[sheet music line 2]
0 0 0 0 1 0   5 5 5 5 6 5   4 4 4 4 5   2 4 3 3

(B) [sheet music line 3]
9   10 9 8 10 9 8   7 4 2 4   3 1 3 5   4 0 2 4

[sheet music line 4]
9 10 9 8 10 9 8   7 4 2 4   9 10 9 8 10 9 8   7 7 7

Go back and play one A Part to end the tune.

Chord Chart

Part A	G	G	D	G
	G	G	D	G
Part B	D A	D	A	D
	D A	D	A	D

I honestly can't say exactly where and when we learned *Belfast Polka*, but I think it was in the 1980s when our band was playing for a local folk dance group. It is commonly played in Ireland and Scotland. In Canada it is used as a Canadian barn dance tune. It is also a popular tune for American line dancing. It's a fun and happy tune played on both sides of the big pond. It's easy! I often use this tune to introduce polkas. Remember, a tune doesn't have to be complex and complicated in order to be a great tune.

LITTLE BLACK DOG CAME TROTTIN' DOWN THE ROAD

Key: G and D
Tuning: dddd or Ddd(d)

Traditional

Source: Luther Davis, (1887-1986) Galax, VA

Go back and play one A Part to end the tune.

Chord Chart				
A Part	G	G	G	G
B Part	D A	D A	D	A D

Can't you just see a sleek and shiny little black dog trottin' down a dusty country lane looking for mischief? He sniffs everything he finds curious and interesting, wags his tail in delight at every new thing, and especially pauses at the pigpen to say hello to his pig friends. I remember this scene from my childhood summers with Granddaddy and Grandma. What a simple life.

Granddaddy, William H. Alger, (1906-1996) holding "Blackie," our little black dog (around 1952).

Two-Key Tunes

PUNCHEON FLOOR

Key: G and D
Tuning: dddd or Ddd(d)

Traditional

Ⓐ
3 2 3 4 5 4 5 6 7 10 7 5 6 7 10 7 10 7 10 5 4

3 2 3 4 5 4 5 6 7 10 7 5 6 7 7 6 5 4 3 4 3 0 | 3 4 3 9 10

Ⓑ
11 9 10 9 8 9 8 7 8 8 9 7 8 8 9 7 8 9 10

11 9 10 9 8 9 8 7 8 8 9 7 8 7 6+ 7 8 7 9 10 | 7 6 5 4

Go back and play one A Part to end the tune.

Chord Chart

Part A	G	G	G	G
	G	G	D	G
Part B	DA	DA	DA	DA
	DA	DA	DA	DA

The earliest historical references to this tune come from 19th century Mississippi. Several variants spread north through the upper south, especially Arkansas, Tennessee, and West Virginia, where it is commonly played today.

A puncheon floor is made of logs cut in half placed round side down on the ground. The flat side up would have been smoothed out to become the floor of the cabin.

Em Tunes

> Ms. Phyllis, I need help! I'm cornfused. This tune looks like it's in the key of G major, but when you play it... Well...It just sounds sooo ... "moody."

> Moody? Are you in the mudddd, AGAIN?!?

Yeah...Kinda...

Hmmm...Let me see if I can explain.
Every major key has a relative minor key which uses the same key signature.

Relative? Like a cousin?

Well...It's more like a brother or sister. The minor scale uses exactly the same notes as the major scale but starts on the 6th tone of the scale instead of the first.

The relative minor for the key of G major is called E minor; it starts on the e (6th tone of the G major scale) and uses all the notes of the G major scale.

E minor Scale   e f# g a b c d e

Fret Number   1 2 3 4 5 6 7 8

G major Scale   g a b c d e f# g

Do you remember changing the drone for the A-ish tunes?

Lucky for us, we use the False Nut or Capo at the first fret for the E minor tunes just like we did for the A-ish tunes. On the Galax dulcimer tuned dddd, the scale starts at the first fret and you have to "play" it without knocking the False Nut out!

OR if you use your <u>DAd dulcimer, capo at the first fret to make EBe. Where the TAB indicates 1 as your fret number, you can strum openly across your dulcimer</u> because the first fret is already pressed down (so fret number one is played open for the EBe minor sound).

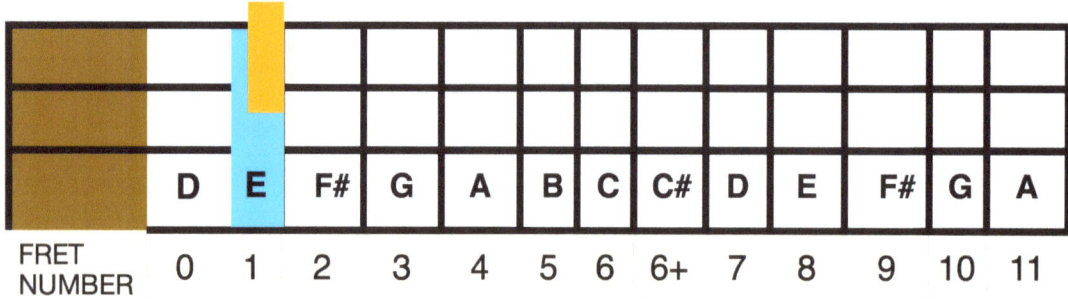

	D	E	F#	G	A	B	C	C#	D	E	F#	G	A
FRET NUMBER	0	1	2	3	4	5	6	6+	7	8	9	10	11

🟨 = False Nut under the d drones to make e drones. The first two open strings will still be dd so you will need to press the strings at the first fret (1) for the ee notes.

🟦 = Capo across all strings to make eeee on a Galax dulcimer or EBe on dulcimer tuned to DAd.
Remember: **When the capo is on the first fret of a dulcimer tuned to DAd, you will already have the first fret pressed down.**

Em Tunes

LANIGAN'S BALL

Key: Em
Tuning: dddd or dddD, use false nut to make e drones or DAd capoed @ 1st fret to make EBe

Traditional Irish Jig

Note: *0 and *3 in the third measure of A Part indicates an open strum on just that one note on the Galax dulcimer or the third fret of the middle string on the capoed DAd dulcimer.

Lanigan's Ball is a great Irish double jig (6/8 time). There are many Irish jigs with lyrics that double as session tunes. This is one of the most widely known and definitely my favorite!

Chord Chart

Part A	Em	Em	D	D
	Em	Em	Em D	Em
Part B	Em	D	Em	D
	Em	D	Em Am	Em

Chorus (B Part)

Six long months I spent up in Dublin,
Six long months doing nothing at all,
Six long months I spent up in Dublin,
Learning to dance for Lanigan's Ball.
I stepped out, I stepped in again,
I stepped out, I stepped in again,
I stepped out, and I stepped in again,
Learning to dance for Lanigan's Ball

Some Lyrics - Verse 1 of 6 (A Part)

In the town of Athol one Jeremy Lanigan
Battered away 'til he hadn't a pound.
His father died and made him a man again
Left him a farm and ten acres of ground.
He gave a grand party to friends and relations,
Who did not forget him when come to the will.
If you'll but listen, I'll make your eyes glisten,
At rows and runctions at Lanigan's Ball.

Em Tunes

SCOLLAY'S REEL

Key: Em
Tuning: dddd or dddD, use false nut to make e drones or DAd capoed @ 1st fret to make EBe

Traditional Irish Reel

Note: *0 and *3 in the fourth measure of A Part and the fourth measure of B Part indicates an open strum on that one note on the Galax dulcimer or the third fret of the middle string on the capoed DAd dulcimer.

Chord Chart

Part A	Em	Em	Em	D
	Em	Em	Em D	Em
Part B	Em	Em	Am Em	D
	Em	Em	Em D	Em

Scollay's Reel (also spelled *Scully's*) is played in both Ireland and Shetland. It is believed by many to be a Shetland version of the Irish set dance *King of the Fair-ies*. It is usually played as an up-tempo dance tune. I believe, however, that the beauty of this tune can best be expressed in a slow to moderate tempo. That is the way Jim and I always play it.

Em Tunes

THE BUTTERFLY

Key: Em
Tuning: dddd or dddD, use false nut
to make e drones or DAd capoed
@ 1st fret to make EBe

Traditional Irish

(A) 5 1 3 1 2   5 1 3 1 2 1 *0/*3   5 1 3 1 2   5 7 7 5 4 2 *0/*3

(B) 5 7 8 9 10   5 7 10 8 7 5 4   5 7 8 9 10 11 12 11 10 8 7 5 4

(C) 5 5 4 3 4 5   5 4 5 7 5 4   5 5 4 3 4 5   5 7 10 8 7 5 4

Chord Chart

A Part	Em D	Em D	Em D	Em D
B Part	Em	Em D	Em	Em D
C Part	Em	Em D	Em	Em D

Note: *0 and *3 in the second and fourth measures of A Part indicates an open strum on that one note on the Galax dulcimer or the third fret of the middle string on the capoed DAd dulcimer.

Ah! *The Butterfly*.

I love this beautiful Irish slip jig (9/8 time). Slip jigs are normally played at very quick tempos for dancing. Tommy Potts (1912-1988), the great iconic fiddler from The Coombe, Dublin, is the source for this tune. Potts had a very improvisational playing style. Our playing of this tune is influenced by the expressive playing of fiddler Kevin Burke who played it almost as a slow air. When we play this tune, we like to vary the tempo as we picture the butterfly moving from place to place sometimes floating on the breeze and other times taking flight.

History

Sandy Parks. Project 367.com

Hoeing The "Hogfiddle" Hills

Maintaining Mountains of Appalachian Dulcimer History

We are so fortunate we do not need to travel into the Appalachian Mountains to learn about the history of the traditional mountain dulcimer and its music. Thankfully, others before us "hoed the hills" removing weeds of misinformation and tending the fragile roots that would grow into branches of knowledge. These folks dug deep into Appalachian culture researching and writing books about firsthand information gleaned from years of travel meeting with, photographing, and interviewing traditional builders and players. I, like many others, learned from them. I also, from the very beginning of my dulcimer journey, traveled through the region meeting and learning from the many great players and makers.

Searching the internet is the modern "research hoe." If you type "Mountain Dulcimer History" in the search box, you may see this statement:

> The Mountain Dulcimer is a true American instrument. It **dates back to the early 1800's**, originating in the Appalachian mountains of southwest Virginia.

Fretted lap zithers such as the German scheitholt, Swedish hummel, the Norwegian langeleik, and the French epinette were the old world ancestors of the Appalachian Mountain Dulcimer.

If you have the opportunity to present a program on the history of the Appalachian Dulcimer, please equip yourself with researched information about the evolution of this wonderful American instrument.

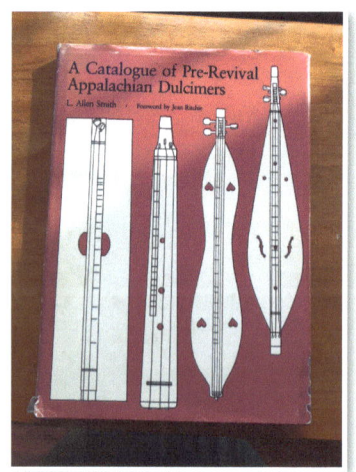

A Catalogue of Pre-Revival Appalachian Dulcimers
1983
L. Allen Smith
University of Missouri Press

The books and articles of Ralph Lee Smith and L. Allen Smith were my go-to sources for historical information. They were among the first to travel to the hills and mountains in search of pre-revival (before 1940) dulcimers and their predecessors.

Ralph wrote a column in the *Dulcimer Players News* from the very beginning of the magazine until his death in 2020. He documented pre-revival dulcimers, their makers, and the players discovered hiby myself and others. Seek out his thorough, scholarly research.

Roddy Moore from Ferrum, Virginia, was a collector of pre-revival mountain dulcimers, folklore and antiques in the Southwest Virginia area and other regions. You can peruse his amazing dulcimer collection housed at the Blue Ridge Institute and Museum, Ferrum College, Ferrum Virginia. Roddy Moore was the collector and curator for this museum and co-authored a wonderful article which you can find online. It outlines much of the history of the Virginia Mountain Dulcimer. You will find it if you search online for *The Magazine Antiques - The Virginia Dulcimer*, July/August, 2013[1].

Peter Ellersten and David Bennett continue to research and disseminate data about the history of the mountain dulcimer. They share their research and cite information gleaned from others before them about newfound pre-revival dulcimers and their predecessors.

Disclaimer: I am not a dulcimer historian. I met and learned from wonderful makers and players, but unfortunately, I did not compile documents with lots of photos and quotes. I have only a few photos and my memory. Only now, as I am writing this, do I realize I am carrying information in my head that really is part of the dulcimer history story. All I really wanted to do was to play like Raymond and learn the tunes and songs to the best of my ability. I fell in love with the Old Virginia dulcimer style of making and playing the dulcimer as it was built and played in Southwest Virginia by Raymond V. Melton and his ancestors. You can find out more about the Meltons and other important dulcimer makers and builders from **Friends of the Mountain Dulcimer,**[2] an online publication dedicated to the preservation and history of playing and building Appalachian mountain dulcimers.

My own Old Virginia Mountain Dulcimer History started at the old Galax Fiddlers Convention in 1976, where I sat beside Raymond Melton observing, listening, and making cassette recordings of his playing.

Felts Park, Galax, Virginia 1977

Raymond V. Melton

Shizuko and Ralph Lee Smith

I played tunes with Ralph Lee Smith and listened to his stories. I decided to leave the writing of history to him and went happily on my way. Our pathways merrily merged on many occasions. The Great Mountain Dulcimer Revival was going strong. New playing styles were evolving in the hands of brilliant players and builders.

1   https://www.themagazineantiques.com
2   https://bppub.net/Friends_Mountain_Dulcimer

Sometimes Roots Get Intertwined, 1978-1980

Creating a circle of dulcimer friends and lots of new experiences filled the years 1978-1980. I am mystified by how my dulcimer journey was intertwined with such wonderful dulcimer friends.

I remained dedicated, some would say stubbornly dedicated, to the traditional Melton-family style of playing. I played tunes with Bonnie Russell and her dad Roscoe, but I was always drawn back to Raymond's playing, undoubtedly the best player of that style. I heard more of his family's instruments were kept in a backroom museum at Harmon's Store in Galax, Virginia. So, I had to visit. The museum is still there as of the writing of this book and is one of our favorite Galax landmarks to visit. The store has nice western style clothing and boots with a large adjoining room in the back which serves as a quaint but fascinating local history museum.

In the Harmon's Store/Museum there are three dulcimers made by Melton family members, dates unknown. The black one has a "sound hole" in the back.

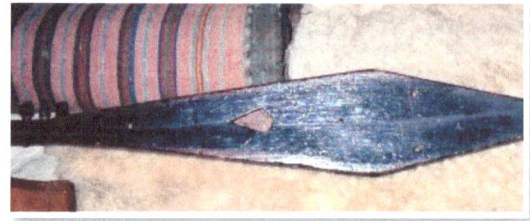

Raymond Melton with members of his band and many dulcimers that he built (photo in the museum).

Roscoe Russell, father of Bonnie Russell, was also a maker and player of the old Galax style dulcimer. His dulcimers have a more exaggerated shape with an elongated head and tailpiece than do Raymond's dulcimers, but Roscoe kept the traditional four equidistant strings of the same gauge tuned to d beside middle C. With the influence of a luthier and good friend, Keith Young, Roscoe started using guitar frets on his dulcimers in the 1970s while Raymond continued with the traditional staple frets. Many people were attracted to Roscoe's post revival dulcimers because of their beauty, and the sound and volume were equal to the Melton dulcimers.

On a recent trip to Galax, I discovered a Russell dulcimer displayed in the back room of Barr's Fiddle Shop, 105 S Main St Galax, Virginia.

Tom Barr, a longtime friend, studied fiddle making with Albert Hash of White Top Mountain, Virgin-ia. Tom has built many fiddles and made dulcimers using an hour-glass shape with the three string set up. He calls them Galax dulcimers because they are built and sold in Barr's Fiddle Shop in Galax. I have played some of Tom's dulcimers; they look and sound really fine but are not the Old Virginia style like those made by the Meltons or the Russells.

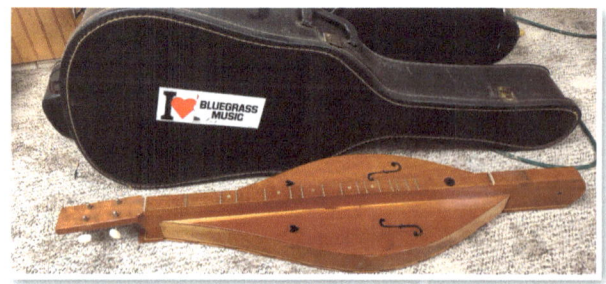

The Roscoe Russell Dulcimer is as long as the guitar case beside it.

In 1978, Jim and I were fortunate to meet White Top Mountain fiddle maker, Albert Hash, and his dulcimer-making daughter, Audrey. We became fast friends and spent an intense period studying instrument making in their basement workshop. Albert helped Jim make a fiddle, and Audrey helped me build a dulcimer using my own interpretation of the Melton Galax design.

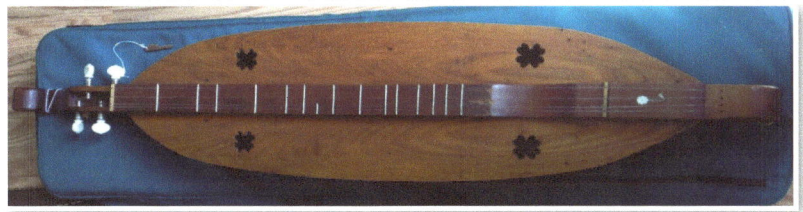

I designed this as my Galax Dulcimer because Raymond was not inclined at that time to build one for me or sell me one of the many he always carried in the trunk of his car. It sounded great, and I won some ribbons with it.

Audrey (right) holds a dulcimer she made using a pattern of a pre-revival dulcimer she and her father found wedged in the wall of an old log cabin near White Top Mountain where they lived. It is a traditional Old Virginia design.

I purchased the dulcimer above from Audrey who made the dulcimer of walnut from a one-hundred-year-old bed. She used only a pocket knife for carving the head (left) of holly wood with rosewood bow and walnut hair. It has the Old Virginia D-shaped tail piece and has holly binding on the edges. Her dulcimers had the familiar three string set up, not the four equidistant strings tuned dddd.

In the *Dulcimer Players News* (Vol. 5, No. 4, Fall 1979), there is an article entitled *DULCIMERS: Virginia Style!* Woody Padgett, who learned to play Galax style dulcimer from Roscoe, wrote the first part of that article about Roscoe's dulcimers. The second part of that article was about Audrey (Hash) Miller written by yours truly. You can view the article online at https://issuu.com/dulcimerplayersnewsinc/stacks.

Audrey taught many people dulcimer making. One was Bob Fletcher who was camped in Grayson Highland State Park during the time that Jim and I were camped there and traversing back and forth to Albert's house. He became curious about where we were going. He introduced himself to us by saying, "I know there's nothing to do around here. Where are you going everyday at 7 and returning late at night?" We told him our good fortune and took him to meet Albert and Audrey.

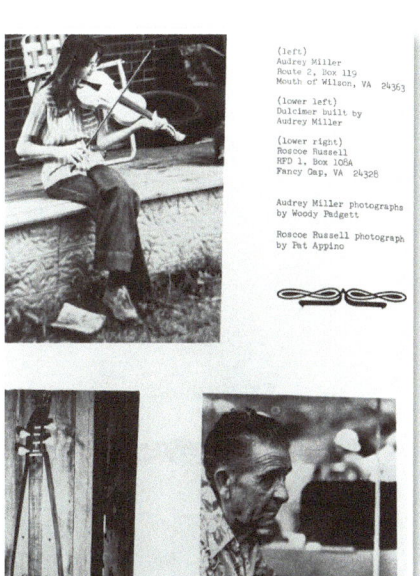

Dulcimer Players News, Fall 1979 (page 32, Vol. 5, o. 4) Used with permission.

History

Then Bob got "bit by the dulcimer bug" and spent his retirement years making Old Virginia style dulcimers using Audrey's pattern. He had a summer dulcimer building workshop in North Carolina and also one at his winter residence in Florida. He sold many dulcimers at the Appalachian State Dulcimer Workshops coordinated by Lois Hornbostel during the 1980s.

You can read more about Bob in *the Dulcimer Players News* Archive at https://issuu.com/dulcimerplayersnewsinc/stacks. Look for 1993, Vol. 9, No. 3, July-September. The article is entitled *A Visit with Bob Fletcher* and was written by Deborah Wilson, Orlando FL. It contains nice photos of some of Bob's dulcimers.

September 15, 1978
Anne, Bob's wife, plays one of the first dulcimers that Bob built.

In an effort to spread a new dulcimer idea, we sent Maddie MacNeil an article about a school project Jim did with his 4th-5th graders. Jim and I created cardboard dulcimer kits in our basement by cutting up cardboard refrigerator and stove boxes. Jim wrote an article about it, and Maddie published it in the *Dulcimer Players News* (DPN), (Vol.4 No.3, Summer 1978, Feedback section, pages 9-10, accessible in the 1978 archives of DPN).

Dulcimer Players News, 1993, (Vol. 9, No. 3, Front Cover) Used with permission from the **Dulcimer Players News.**

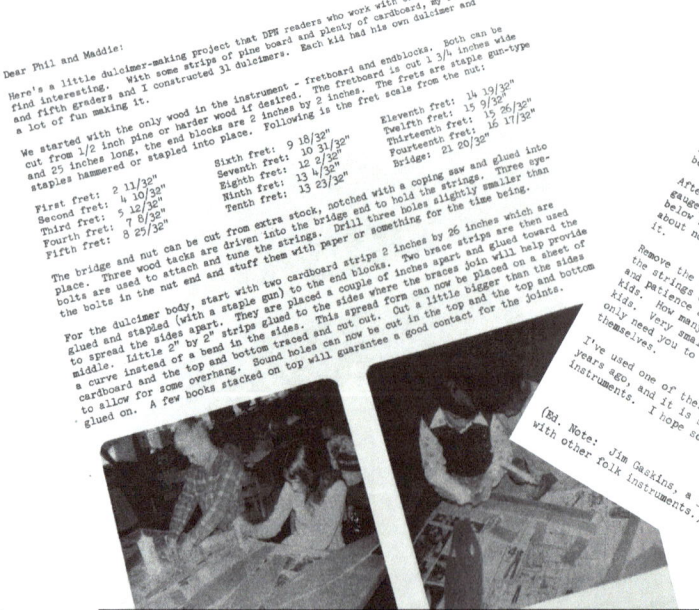

Jim's letter to **the Dulcimer Players News**, 1978. Used with permission from **Dulcimer Players News**.

History

German Hummels

I believe enough evidence now suggests that the dulcimer was born in Old Virginia (now West Virginia and Virginia) before the Civil War. The instrument then evolved as makers incorporated their own ideas into the design of their respective dulcimers. The early settlers migrated through Old Virginia to the West and the South. Since communities were more or less isolated, the dulcimers developed various shapes and tunings generally corresponding to the different geographical areas.

The Great Philadelphia Wagon Road through The Great Valley of Virginia was the gateway through which German settlers carried scheitholts and hummels from Pennsylvania down through the southern Appalachians. Those instruments were similar to these from my hummel collection.

I purchased this hummel from Wilfried Ulrich, a copy of a Frisian hummel from 1800. The lyre sound hole is copied from a hummel made around 1800. The *four flowers* sound hole was copied from a viola da gamba. This one has a French epinette fret scale. An original hummel would not have had those extra frets on the drone side of the fretboard and no 6+ fret under the dddd strings.

TUNING CHART FOR HUMMEL

Note	String Gauge
G - an octave below the G—	.048 wound (or .049/.050)
D below middle C	.032 wound
D below middle C	.032 wound
G below middle C	.020 wound
d beside middle C	.012
d	
d	
d	

Interestingly, the first four strings of the old hummels were the same gauge and tuned to dddd like the old Melton style Galax dulcimers. Is this where the Meltons got their tuning?

I believe so.

History

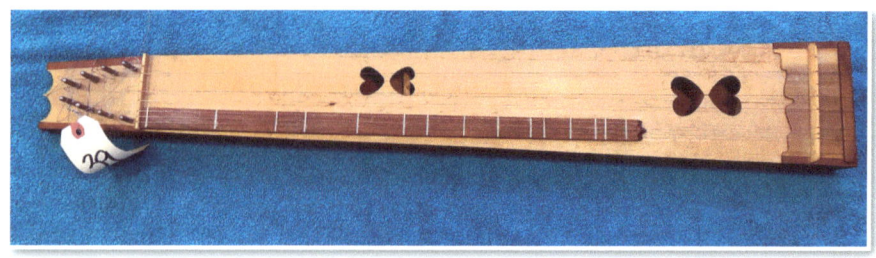

I purchased this copy of a hummel from the estate auction of Patty Looman (1925-2012), West Virginia dulcimer player, historian, and teacher. It has the same tuning as described on page 83. It has the harpsichord-style tuning pins which need to be tuned with a special wrench.

This hummel with harpsichord-style tuning pins was made by a longtime friend, Ken Bloom, and uses the same tuning as on page 83. I purchased this from Ken at the Crooked Road Dulcimer Festival, Ferrum College, Ferrum, Virginia, where he and I were both instructors.

I'm tired of all this corn-y hist'ry! Color me! OR Let's play a game!

JUST FOR FUN! Do you remember this game called *Pig in a Pen*? We called it *Dot-to-Dot* and played it with friends in class to fill time while waiting for others to finish their work. It took a while to fill up a page with dots, and it kept us quiet!

Swinettes / Bedpost Scheitholts

The German settlers brought instruments known as scheitholts and hummels into the Shenandoah Valley of Virginia via The Great Wagon Road (now Route 11). In the early 1980s I met Junior Davis from Linville, Virginia, only a few miles west of Route 11 in Rockingham County. He was displaying his instruments, fiddles and swinettes as well as other creations at the Blue Ridge Community College Annual Arts and Crafts Festival. His swinette was actually a copy of a "bedpost" scheitholt found by someone in western Rockingham County and taken to Mr. Davis for him to copy. I have two of them left in my collection. I sold one to Ralph Lee Smith, gave one to a luthier friend who was building dulcimers at the time, and traded one for a dulcimer that was made in Shenandoah, Virginia.

Ralph Lee Smith (1927-2020) was a longtime friend and my go-to source for dulcimer history. I introduced Ralph to Junior Davis's work which was written up in our local newspaper, *the Daily News Record* (November 18, 1983). Ralph visited Junior in 1984 and included a few paragraphs of information about him and his swinettes in the first edition of *The Story of the Dulcimer* (published by Crying Creek Publishers).

At right, you see this picture of Junior Davis from *The Story of the Dulcimer*, 1986 (first edition, page 59). When I was doing a presentation at the Ferrum College Crooked Road Dulcimer Festival, I asked Ralph if I could use something from his book in my slideshow presentation. He said, "You can use anything from my book anytime you want."

In the second edition of *The Story of the Dulcimer,* (The University of Tennessee Press, Knoxville, 2016, pages 66-67), Ralph included an additional photo of a swinette and a cigar box fiddle which Junior had made. If you don't have a copy of that book, pick one up. Junior Davis was the last traditional builder of scheitholts found in Rockingham County, Virginia.

Figure 102: Junior Davis, 76-year-old fiddle and "swinette" (scheitholt) maker of Linville, Rockingham County, Shenandoah Valley, Virginia, shown holding one of his swinettes. Photo taken in 1984.

History

Pictured below is one of my Junior Davis scheitholts in its handcrafted case. Junior dubbed this instrument a swinette because he said, "It sounded like a pig scratching itself on a fencepost." The top photo shows the view from above, and the bottom photo shows the side view.

The sound box of my second Davis swinette (below) is made of yellow pine, and including the bedpost finials, measures 43" in length. The vibrating string length (VSL) is 25 1/4". The top, back and sides are 30" long x 3 1/4" wide x 1/4" thick. The end blocks are 3 1/2" x 3 1/4" x 1 1/4." The bedpost finial head is 5 1/4" long, and the tail bedpost finial is 4 1/4".

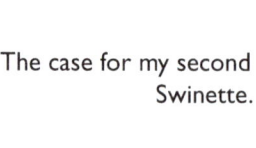

The handle on the case with JUNIOR DAVIS stamped into the wood beside the handle.

The case for my second Swinette.

History

The Appalachian Mountain Dulcimer: An American Instrument

Ok, ok, ok....
I'm not real!
But those Germans were real!
They brought real hummels, scheitholts, and
OINK, OINK, OINK ...
Ms. Phyllis,
What does that have to do with dulcimers?

Quit distracting me with all that oinking!

Not all immigrants who came down The Great Wagon Road were German. There were also Scotch-Irish, Welsh, and English immigrants. As more people moved into the valley and the mountain areas, the German zithers, hummels and scheitholts were transformed into a brand new American instrument called the mountain dulcimer (delcimore, hogfiddle, lap dulcimer).

It is believed that the Scotch-Irish immigrants in the mountainous areas along The Great Wagon Road with their affinity for bagpipe drones, adapted the German instruments creating this new instrument.

1. They added a raised fretboard for frets (usually hand bent staples) rather than putting the frets into the body of the instrument.
2. They reduced the number of melody strings to one or two and drones on one middle and one bass string.
3. They created new body shapes.

The most common shapes found in Virginia were simple and easy to create with the limited tools available at the time.

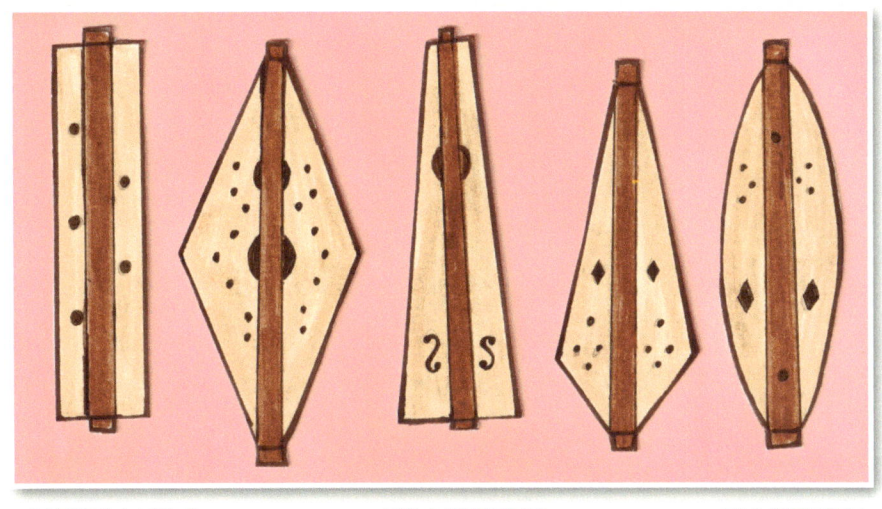

RECTANGLE   TRAPEZOID   ELLIPTICAL
DIAMOND   KITE

History

More and more immigrants came pouring down The Great Wagon Road. Quite a number of settlers migrated across the ridge and valley topography of what is now West Virginia. Gerald Milnes devotes Chapter 11, *Harps, Waterswivels, and Fence Scorpions* of his book, **Play of a Fiddle**, to documenting the pre-revival dulcimers (made before 1940) found in West Virginia. Many families crossed the mountains directly from Pennsylvania at various points along The Great Wagon Road. Milnes states "…all of the old fretted zithers from Pennsylvania and Virginia as well as examples I have seen in Geenbrier, Hardy, Randolph, and Summers Counties in West Virginia, have diatonic fret intervals" (page 138). Milnes includes photos of the old West Virginia dulcimers. The makers there developed attractive, subtle variations in the shape and tuning of their dulcimers.

Old Virginia is outlined by the blue line on the map below. The black dotted line indicates where Virginia was divided on June 20, 1863 to make two states, West Virginia and Virginia.

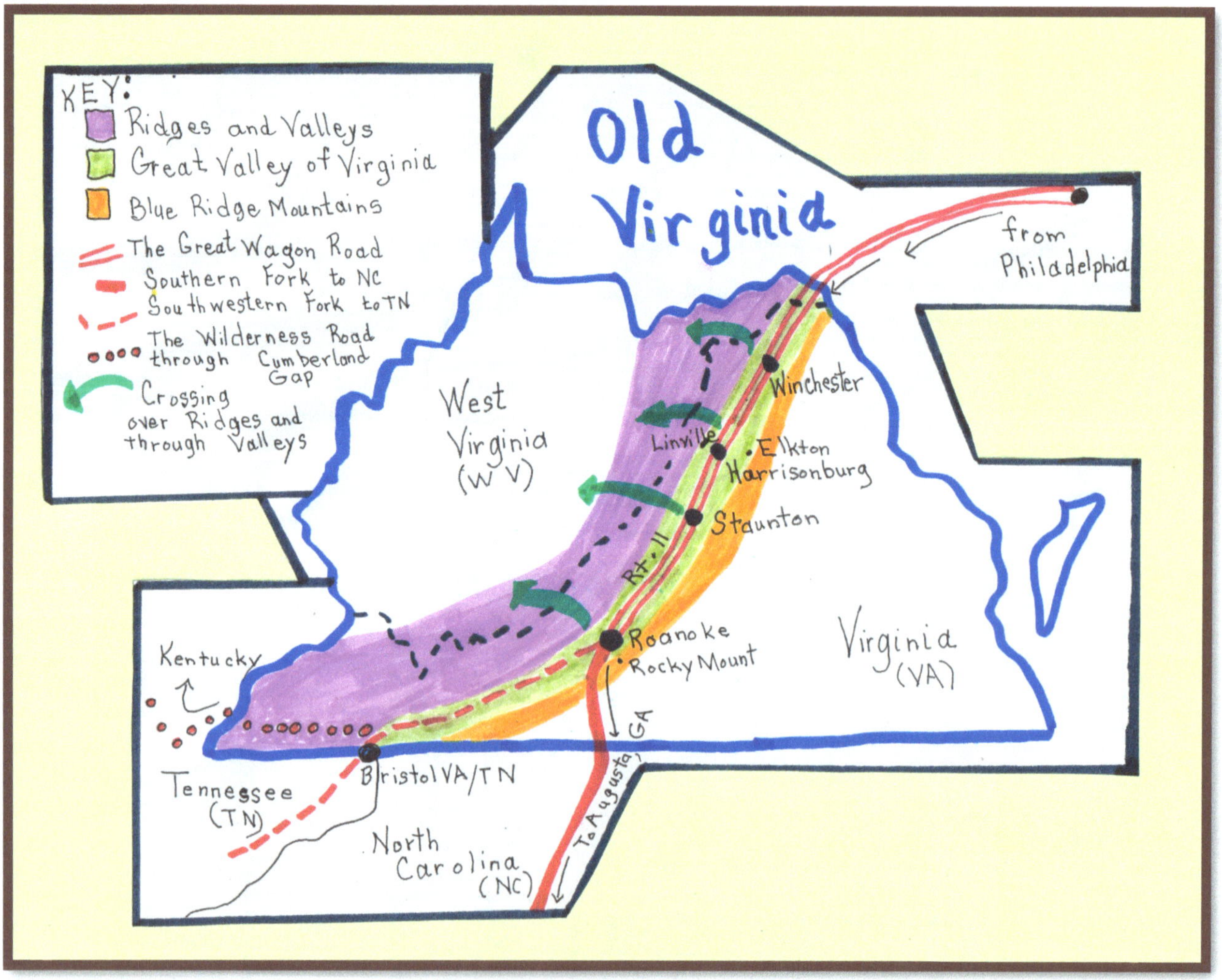

Near Roanoke, The Great Wagon Road split. The southern fork continued into North Carolina and was called The Carolina Road. The southwestern fork led into The New River Valley and on through Bristol, Virginia then it continued into Tennessee. At Bristol, The Wilderness Road forked off to the west and through the Cumberland Gap. This allowed settlers to enter into Kentucky and the Ohio Valley.

Luthiers became more experienced and had access to or created their own tools for shaping and bending wood. Makers put their creative ideas into practice and other dulcimer shapes evolved from these Old Virginia shapes.

Hour-glass and teardrop shapes found in Kentucky, much of North Carolina, and Tennessee were beautiful and graceful looking instruments. Those dulcimer shapes became the most prevalent and sought after shapes during the dulcimer revival which started in the early 1960s.

In the fall of 1973 I saw a dulcimer made by Bob Mize. It was a beauty! I could play it with ease. I ordered one on the spot!

My Bob Mize Dulcimer, 1974

But as you already know, I was truly bitten by the Old Virginia styles!

Below is my collection as of 1980 when I first got my Galax dulcimer from Raymond Melton.

Photo by Sandy Parks. Project 367.com

Galax Dulcimer Makers

One of the Virginia shapes that survived from the early to mid 1800s up to the present day is what has become known as the Galax Dulcimer. This term was given to cover a type of dulcimer shape and playing style from the southwestern area of Virginia. This particular style of dulcimer making and playing was preserved over many decades within one extended family in and around the area of Galax, Virginia, the Meltons. Prior to and during the first 50 years of the Galax Fiddlers Convention they kept this style alive in the string band tradition while taking all of the top prizes in dulcimer competitions there. This dulcimer style, one of the oldest in the history of mountain dulcimers, predates the modern dulcimer revival.

If you are searching for a Galax Dulcimer, please look for these specific characteristics:

- elliptical shape
- a double bottom (which Raymond left off in his later years because he said his instruments were loud enough without it)
- a one-piece head-fretboard-tailpiece combo that is hollow with a hole drilled through the strumming area and generally at the upper end between the first and second frets as well.
- no strum hollow (carved out area under the strings in the strumming area) on the fretboard
- D-shaped tailpiece with a hole or holes drilled through it
- four equidistant strings of the same gauge (.010)
- 6.5 fret (Raymond Melton was most likely the first person to put this on the mountain dulcimer.)

Pieces of a Galax Dulcimer ready for assembly. Photo courtesy of John Knopf.

Knopf Dulcimers

John Knopf, Luthier
35135 June Drive
Westland, Michigan 48186
(734) 722-5931
knopfjc1@juno.com
https://knopfdulcimer.webs.com

Left: John in his workshop.

Right: The inside of one of John's Melton-style dulcimers.

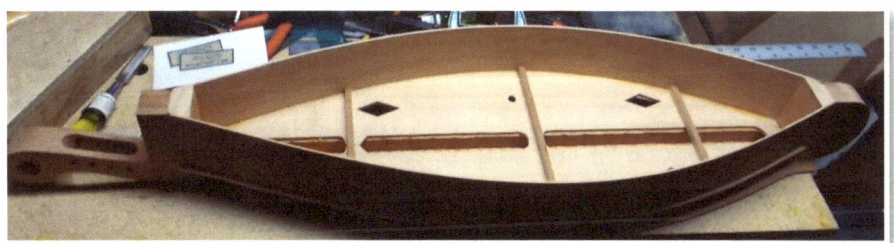

Lori Lineweaver's Beautiful Ben Seymour

Melton Style Dulcimer

Kudzu Patch Dulcimers

Ben Seymour, Luthier
2142 Coxe Road
Tryon, North Carolina 28782
(828) 863-4384
kudzupatch@gmail.com
http://www.kudzupatch.net/galax.htm

Double D Dulcimers

Don Neuhauser has made many Galax style dulcimers. I recently found one for sale on the internet. If you can find one, you are very fortunate indeed!

History

Home Now

Before the European immigrants moved into the Great Valley of Virginia, the original inhabitants of Old Virginia had been here 10,000-20,000 years. Those Native Americans had been cleared out of the valley through the use of force and treaties for resettlement in other regions of the growing United States. Many residents of the Shenandoah Valley carry within themselves DNA from both the original inhabitants and the immigrants. I am one of those residents.

As a child I would ask my dad about the "others" who came before us and what he answered inspired me to write *Home Now* in 1996.

I was born in my grandparents' house on the hill, down the hill a little ways was the pig house and pig pen. We always had butchering day on Thanksgiving and that gave us enough meat to last for the year until the next Thanksgiving. The leaning shed on the left is where the chickens roosted, and the large building on the right housed the corn crib and tools. The milk cow was fenced in the lot to the right of the large building and had a lean-to shed for shelter. There was a large field to the right where we grew corn for the animals and for grinding cornmeal. I took this photo of Dad in 1968. Over time only the outbuildings fell into disrepair from non-use.

After Dad passed, I found this photo (above) of his little family in his wallet.

Phyllis and I deliberately left off the numbers and strumming arrows. Try your hand at adding them to the score.

Shh! Don't tell anyone, but little Phyllis liked to play with the chickens and the pigs.

HOME NOW

Phyllis Gaskins

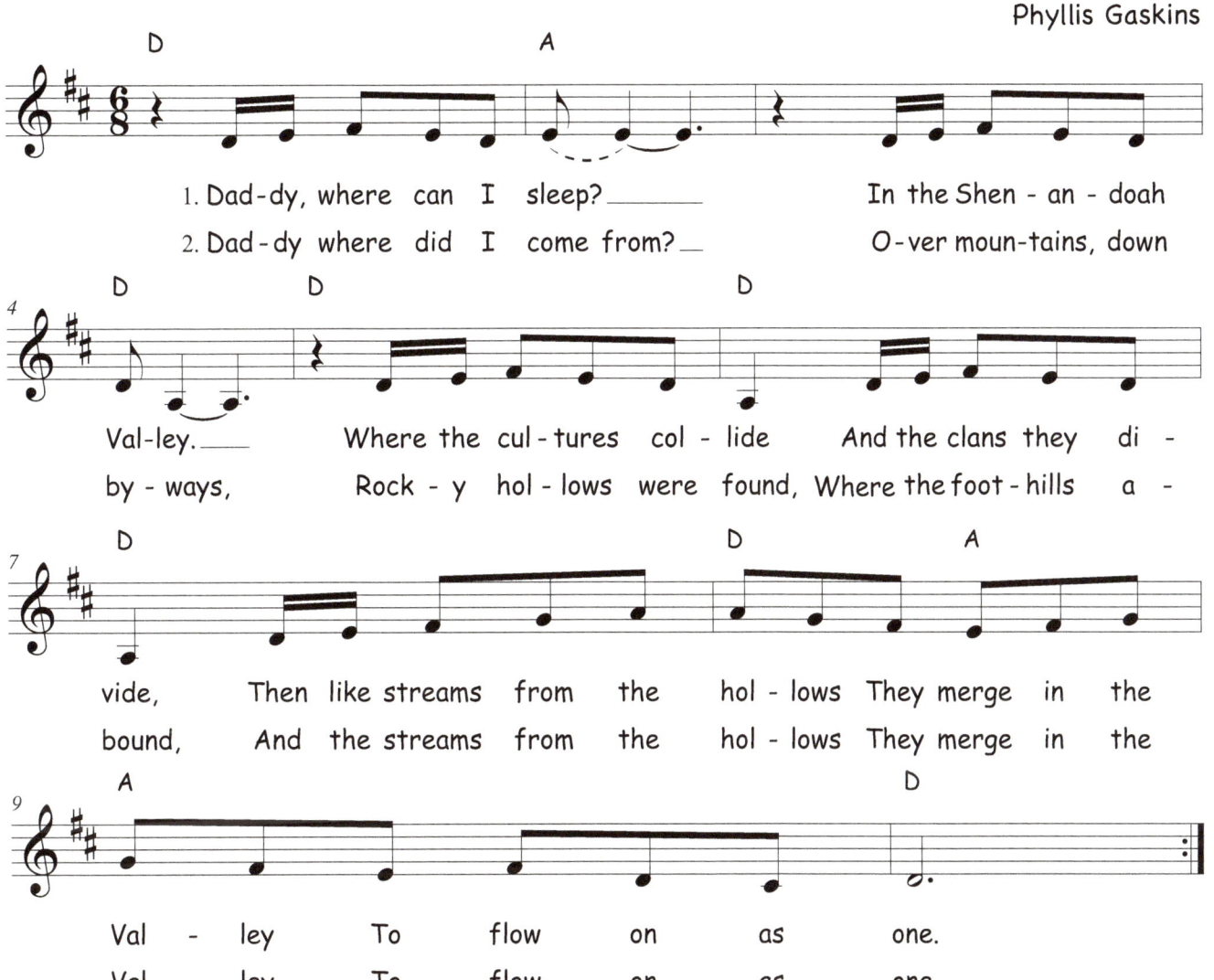

3. Daddy, who were the first?
In the Valley stood wigwams,
Children played river games,
Their fathers gave us their name,
And like streams from the hollows
They merged in the Valley
To flow on as one.

4. Daddy, who came before us?
From the island called Eire,
Oh, the Scotch-Irish might,
Filled with dreams of their rights,
Came like streams from the hollows
To merge in the Valley
And flow on as one.

5. Daddy, when can I go there?
To the island called Eire,
Where the sweet Shannon flows,
Like our own Shenandoah,
From the streams in the hollows,
To merge in the Valley
And flow on as one.

6. Daddy, are we at home now?
With the hay in the barn,
We have all done our best,
We can lie down to rest,
And like the streams from the hollows
We'll merge in the Valley
To flow on as one.

Acknowledgements

Jim

Like a '52 Chevy you're a classic!
Taking life one year at a time!
Lots of dents and scratches,
A little rust on the side,
But, honey, that's just fine!
One year at a time.

We're on our way in #52,
Lots of music and travels behind,
Studied the "fiddlin' past"
Learned music from heroes,
Heard stories,
Should have taken better notes!
Your mem'ry holds it all!
We drive head-on!
One year at a time.

Traveled sigogglin roads
In that '76 chevy pickup truck
With the topper on the back!
Summer heat and thunderstorms,
Tailgate picking, canopy flapping,
Voracious fiddling, banjo strumming,
Dulcimer humming,
Dust and mud!
Oh, honey, wasn't it grand!
One year at a time.

Here we are in '22!
Celebrating 52!
Older than that Chevy Truck!
Four leaf clovers brought us luck.
Music took us far and wide,
Glad to have you by my side!
One year at a time.

Let's go "fidl'cimer-ing"!

Many thanks to Jim for all of his help with this book!

Thanks for all researching, memories, date checking, editing, and all the moral support!

Lori Lineweaver

Thank you for the countless hours of learning the tunes and checking the arrows and numbers.

I believe you've got the Galax noter/strum thing down! Love playing with you, you are a very special person.

Alzbeta Springer

Dear Dulcimer Daughter,

Thanks for saying, "That's not how you're playing it," when you looked at new tune notation.

Dear Friends, Students, and Readers All,

I am so thankful for all of the blessings of the dulcimer muse guiding me through the days and years of my life. My dulcimer and I have shared love of tradition and music with you, and you have mirrored that love by sharing with others. Through good times and bad may you find solace in music. May it open new vistas for you on life's journey.

Dulcimercifully yours,

Phyllis

> Videos of Jim and Phyllis playing many of the tunes in this book are available on their Vimeo Showcase.
>
> Tunes for You
> https://vimeo.com/showcase/7823477

If you haven't seen Phyllis's first book of Galax Dulcimer tunes or all of her fine CD recordings, you can preview them on her website: https://virginiadulcimer.com.

www.ingramcontent.com/pod-product-compliance
Lightning Source LLC
Chambersburg PA
CBHW041537220426
43663CB00002B/59